SCOTTISH CANAL CRIMES

SCOTTISH CANAL CRIMES

Murder and Mayhem on Scotland's Towpaths

1800-1950

T A STEWART

First published 2021
by Rymour Books
45 Needless Road,
PERTH
PH20LE

© T A Stewart 2021
ISBN 978-1-8384052-6-7

http://www.rymour.co.uk

cover and book design by Ian Spring
printed by Imprint Digital, Exeter, Devon

A CIP record for this book
is available from the British Library

The paper used in this book is approved
by the Forest Stewardship Council

CONTENTS

INTRODUCTION   9

Chapter One: NO FIXED ABODE   14

Chapter Two: SAFE AS HOUSES   46

Chapter Three: SINS OF THE PEOPLE   70

ILLUSTRATIONS

Chapter Four: WOMEN BEWARE   95

Chapter Five: A HIGHLANDER ABROAD   120

Chapter Six: RUTHLESS TRADERS   140

SOURCES   158

INDEX   164

ILLUSTRATIONS

Between pages 88 and 95.

1.   Port Dundas, 1950s.
2.   Causewayend Bridge on the Union Canal.
3.   Reward notice published in the *Caledonian Mercury*.
4.   Explosives expert Colonel Vivian Dering Majendie.
5.   The Forth and Clyde Canal at Maryhill.
6.   The northern end of the Caledonian Canal.
7.   The Kintore Murder.
8.   The Inn at Ratho.
9.   Artist's depiction of the murder of Jeannie Seaton.
10. Edinburgh surgeon Dr Joseph Bell.
11. The Linlithgow and Stirlingshire Hunt.
12. Hillside at Preston Fields.
13. Union Canal engineer Hugh Baird.
14. Record of the death from hanging of Bell McMenemy.

MAP OF SCOTLAND'S CANALS

Inverness

1

Aberdeen

2

3

4
5
6   7
Glasgow   Edinburgh

Key to Canals
1. Aberdeenshire
2. Caledonian
3. Crinan
4. Forth and Clyde
5. Monkland
6. Paisley
7. Union

ACKNOWLEDGEMENTS

I'd like to thank the many people who have, in their different ways, helped me to chronicle historical canal crime. Members of staff were ever-willing to assist with unearthing documents held in our archival treasure troves: the National Records of Scotland, the National Library of Scotland, the Mitchell Library, Stirling Council Archives and further afield, the Archives of Ontario in Canada. In the earliest phase of my research, Sybil Cavanagh, the former local history librarian at Linlithgow, and Carol Morgan, of the Institution of Civil Engineers in London, drew on their expertise to help locate important sources.

Special thanks go to Rymour Books, particularly to Ian Spring for his unwavering enthusiasm and his work and skill in the art of publication. I thank Susanne Crichton, Simon McGhee and Veronica Sañudo, whose advice and attentiveness helped make the writing of this book noticeably easier. For superb technical support and more I'm grateful, as always, to Douglas Knapp. I thank Tom Lynch for rewarding historical conversation and a specific insight on boatmen. Suzy Berry and Max Crawford stepped in wonderfully, at the drop of a hat, during the geographical restrictions of lockdown. Thanks to Andrew MacDonald for the photo of Port Dundas, 1950 on the cover and to Max for the back cover photo of the lock by Temple Gas Works.

I warmly thank all family and friends who gave practical and moral support, especially Rosemary, Jane, Fiona and Deborah. The kindest encourager from times past was undoubtedly my mother Moira. I thank Michael, Sylvie and Patrick for their ongoing encouragement, for their patience and willingness to join me on field trips with sun hats, waterproofs or thermals as necessary, and their uncanny flair for finding humour in unexpected places. This book is dedicated to the four of them.

Thérèse Stewart, 2021

INTRODUCTION

Scotland's canals have attracted criminals of every stripe since the Forth and Clyde opened in 1790. Assailants and murderers, kidnappers and terrorists, burglars and grave robbers have all been drawn to the water to practise their black arts. This book investigates some of the most intriguing incidents that took place from the dawn of the nineteenth century to the year 1950, the period that might broadly be described as the heyday of the waterways. Since canal crime is not just a historical phenomenon, many of the insights to be gleaned from the heyday remain relevant. In 27 cases, this book explores why Scotland's canals have so often served as the perfect setting for crime. Is there something about the linear nature of the canal that offers a particularly suitable locus? Have calculating criminals been drawn to the banks with a view to carrying out their plans, or did they just happen to be there when carrying out an act of violence or plunder?

In the immediate aftermath, the perpetrator's over-riding concern is the disposal of evidence. The canal serves his or her needs well in that respect. Every year, scores of poignant reports appeared in the Scottish press revealing the discovery of yet another body in a canal in the Highlands or Lowlands. In the case of deceased adults, it was all too easy to dismiss the death as a result of lost footing in the dark, since canal paths were well used in the twilight hours. Men or women of lower-class status were commonly assumed to have been drunk, regardless of whether evidence for this existed or not. Explanations of the misadventurous variety were grasped at with enthusiasm, since the idea that a large number of people had chosen death by drowning was unpalatable. The fact that apparently accidental deaths seemed to be more common during wartime points towards at least some of these being suicides. However, in other cases a crime had clearly been committed, not least on those occasions when it was witnessed. A court case would generally ensue and the circumstances would be aired, triggering widespread fascination. Murders that took place on the banks, as opposed to those by drowning, tended to be violent in character.

Perhaps the greatest scandal is the number of deceased infants who were found in the water. Over 110 such discoveries are reported in Scottish newspapers during the heyday, which surely makes the phenomenon one of Scotland's most uncomfortable secrets. The idea that a mother had dropped the baby through clumsiness seldom served as a credible account of events. It was possible that a child had passed away of natural causes and the canal water was used as a tomb to avoid burial fees. However, appeals for information tended to be headed "PRESUMED INFANTICIDE". Evidence supporting the presumption might take the form of a ligature tied about the neck, or a rag stuffed into the mouth. Even without the advances of today's forensic science, the fact that it had been a deliberate act was often painfully obvious. While the explanation for many infant deaths would remain a mystery, strong social ties during the period made it difficult for a woman to conceal a pregnancy without arousing suspicion. In these identified cases, the events leading to a child's demise would almost inevitably come to light in court. The public reaction would be condemnation or pity or an uneasy brew of both.

House robberies tend to involve advance planning and it is clear that the opportunities offered by the waterway were not lost on some would-be thieves. For instance, one gang of robbers was able to observe the comings and goings at a country house at their leisure before jemmying the door, then making off with the loot by boat. During the era when the canals were busy with trading and passenger vessels, canalside houses made for a soft target. Towards the end of the heyday, one amateurish trio used a canal bank to hide a safe they had stolen because it had proved impossible to open. As their desperation grew, the plan they came up with proved to be as crazy as it was dangerous. A different type of plunder was carried out by cunning business people who exploited the trading opportunities that were part and parcel of the waterways. For this, careful planning and a veneer of respectability had to be employed.

Some incidents took place there because the location was quiet and dark. A towpath was much more secluded than a town pavement and allowed for a sprint round a bend or a dive into the bushes. By far the most popular canal locus was close to or beneath a bridge—the sort of setting thriller writers dream about. This served as an excellent sort of spot because the risk of being seen was lessened by the structure and its shadows, and the sound of placing something in the water would be muffled. The bridge also provided an easy route to and from the scene. Some moving bridges turned out to be manned, however, or a passer-by could appear at exactly the wrong moment.

Until now, women have largely been invisible in canal history, overwhelmed by images of men as heroic pioneers grappling to tame a wayward landscape; ingenious engineers and financial adventurers whose drive is to be celebrated. Yet we know that canal ventures in Scotland, with the exception of the Caledonian, were undertaken for the purpose of personal enrichment rather than public benefit, since many of the backers were involved in trade that sought new markets. Among the labourers, the excavation work cost lives. We also know that the entrepreneurs tended to be wildly optimistic, with running out of money a regular feature of canal-building. A canal might prove to be too short (the Union), too ambitious (the Caledonian), too hastily-constructed (the Crinan), or be quickly outmoded by rail routes (the Lowland ones and the Aberdeenshire). Women come to the fore when we look at canal crime and related social history. We start to see that they worked on the banks, in mills and other industrial works, and often used the canal towpaths when seeking employment—a good rule of thumb being that where there was water-power, there might be work. Female domestic servants who had lost their position swelled the ranks of towpath wanderers who were liable to become a victim or a perpetrator. Whatever the woman's role, though, it was likely to be stereotyped. When Bell McMenemy was hanged in the autumn of 1828, a huge crowd looked on, fascinated by her reputation as a professional femme fatale.

In recent years the canals have enjoyed a pristine touristic reputation, with images of horses contentedly pulling boats by verdant pastures. This misrepresents how things really were. Canal development then, as now, came with the cost of increasing pollution and landscape blight and ushered in a physical environment suited to murky deeds, especially during the hours when respectable folk sleep. The Howgate Head in Glasgow had fine credentials in this regard, having been associated with the grim reaper before it became the Monkland Canal basin. Two groups of covenanters met their end there in the 1600s and in the 1760s the spot was adopted as Glasgow's official execution site. A particularly gruesome spectacle was the execution of Hugh Bilsland, a much-wanted man who was finally caught robbing a surgeon in Argyle Street, and hordes descended in 1767 for the novelty of seeing a woman hanged. Agnes Dougal had taken the life of her nine-year-old daughter, Joanna, to oblige a potential suitor and such was the outrage, the condemned woman had to be escorted under armed guard. Six executions had taken place by the time the Howgate Head was claimed for the Monkland Canal and it would remain a place with unpleasant associations. The basin swiftly became the stamping ground of footpads who preyed on lone passers-by.

For more than a century, the ill-treatment of horses working on Scotland's canals was a matter of routine. In the mid-nineteenth century a few brave souls began to speak out against it, though prosecutions did not occur until the late nineteenth century. Violent acts, whether against humans or animals, seemed most unexpected when they took place in the prettiest rural spots on the Highland canals. Every one of Scotland's waterways features in the annals of crime, even the lesser-known Paisley, Aberdeenshire and Monklands Canals. The darker side of canal history has lain largely undisturbed in other respects too. Without slavery money the Forth and Clyde, the Union, the Monkland and the Crinan might never have existed, since they were part-financed by tobacco lords and others who profited from the trade*. That ignominy is beyond the scope of this book, as are the accidental drownings, apparent suicides and petty crimes such as passenger boat pick-pocketing. Incidents had a habit of happening on board, boatmen having a reputation for being a parcel of rogues. They worked on a Sunday, making them non-attenders at church or chapel, and the itinerant life meant little or no education. The rope-cutting knives that were tools of their trade did lead to tragedy.

Boatmen were often very young, worked for hours in a confined space, and frequently had alcohol problems. Many were former canal labourers who were regarded as the lowest in society, reflecting the common prejudice against Irishmen and Roman Catholics. The most famous example of such labourers were the serial murderers, Burke and Hare. This book doesn't describe their widely-recounted West Port murders, but sets out to clarify the limited extent of their involvement in canal crime. Of more interest here is the sensational body-snatching case of the Latona and the fate of John McGraddy, an Irish boatman who paid a disproportionate price for his involvement in an armed robbery. The aim is to open the door on a subject that has barely been explored. Informed by evidence from newspaper reports, court papers and correspondence, I have done my utmost to ignore the myths and tourist-friendly tall-tales. The facts are more interesting by far.

* Numerous slave profiteers financed Scotland's canals. Examples are Sir Lawrence Dundas of Kerse (Forth and Clyde); William Cunningham of Lainshaw (Union); Alexander Spiers of Elderslie (Monkland); Sir Archibald Edmonstone (Crinan).

CHAPTER ONE: NO FIXED ABODE

Out in the Cold

In August 1864, a group of young men headed for the area known as the New Pig-iron Basin at Port Dundas, Glasgow. There was nothing unusual in this. Once the workers had gone and the light was dim, homeless men often would steal into the industrial maze along the Forth and Clyde Canal. These figures would move among the shadows, seeking warmth and shelter in the complex of sheds and outbuildings, refineries, warehouses and granaries where chemicals, dyes, glass, cotton, fire bricks and iron goods were processed during the day. The police knew that the Port Dundas basin attracted more than its share of nocturnal drifters. A handful of such people would be admitted to the small police office in Maitland Street to stay for one night only—under police protection, as it was known. Others would look to kip down on empty berthed boat or in an outbuilding. The coke manufacturing company John Watson and Son were aware that small groups of open-air sleepers were drawn at night to their kilns, situated right on the edge of the canal. The men were lured by the comforting warmth that was given out by the huge furnaces that were kept running at all hours. Far from being sympathetic to these itinerants, Watsons took exception to what they saw as trespassing on their property. The company had asked Maitland Street officers to patrol the kilns at least once during their night-time beat, with the instruction that any person found sleeping there should be ordered to move along.

Eighteen-year-old James Wilson found himself on the streets after falling out with his aunts, Catherine and Eliza, who lived in the city's Whitehall Street. Wilson liked to describe himself as an apprentice baker, but in truth his was a hand-to-mouth existence. He could get only intermittent work on the stalls at the Glasgow Bazaar in Candleriggs, where he would undertake any errands or odd jobs he could pick up. For about three weeks following the family argument, he had been going to Watson's kilns and sleeping in the company of other destitute young men. On the night of Thursday 24th he once again headed there, carefully threading his way along the narrow path that ran alongside the canal, made more dangerous by the stones and bricks that were strewn across it. Large barrows had been parked beside the roofs of the kilns and in one barrow, three young men were already slumbering in the warmth. Wilson clambered up a ladder leaning against the side of the kiln and settled down into a second barrow, which was empty.

He had met the trio before. They were George Hunter, a bottle factory worker who had recently been put out of work, and two former apprentice moulders, Angus Campbell and John Broadfoot. All three were younger than he was—about fifteen or sixteen years of age, he thought. That night Broadfoot was dressed in distinctive white clothes that showed up his sturdy build in the moonlight. He had served his moulder's apprenticeship with Edrington and Son at the Phoenix Ironworks, then worked with Law and Company of Port Dundas until that came to an end. He could no longer pay for a roof over his head in nearby Bishop Street and his parents' recent move from Anderston, Glasgow, to Fisherrow near Musselburgh had left him with no option other than to sleep outdoors for three consecutive nights. All the men were aware that the police were likely to appear on patrol so George Hunter lay keeping an eye out. At one point in the recent past the police had intensified their tough stance towards rough sleepers at the kilns by apprehending anyone found slumbering there, although on the date in question the policy was simply to move them on.

Wilson was tired and fell asleep. He was disturbed at 2am by the uncomfortable sensation of a policeman's baton prodding his chest. He got to his feet quickly and saw that there were two officers. One was about thirty years with sandy side-whiskers and a north of Scotland accent. The older officer, the one who had prodded him, demanded: "Why the hell are you lying here?" Angus Campbell was poked on the leg by the younger man. The youths got up and ran away along the kiln wall and clambered down to the basin, then turned a corner. They set off in a northerly direction straight towards the water, with the policemen in hot pursuit. Wilson glanced back to see the sandy-whiskered officer catch up with Broadfoot in the narrow, rubble-filled space between the kiln and canal, yelling: "You bugger, I'll drown ye." The officer then pushed Broadfoot in the middle of the back with his truncheon, launching him into the canal. Wilson saw and heard the splash. Alarmed, he ascended one of the kiln ladders and looked down. Broadfoot was struggling in the water. The constable had gone to the neighbouring bank and got down on his knees. Whether the officer was trying to rescue the boy or subject him to further torment it wasn't possible to see.

Fearful of being caught, Wilson climbed down and crossed the bridge to the other bank. From a hiding place on the north bank he silently watched the policemen coming over the bridge towards them. An animated conversation was going on between the officers and grew increasingly heated as it went on. The older man remarked that he thought something had made a splash in the canal and received the reply that one of the boys had ended up in the canal. The other said: "God almighty, do you tell me that? Did you give him a push into the canal?" The sandy-whiskered man said: "Do you think I'm daft?" and added that it had been the lad wearing the white clothes. The older man said he would go and report what had happened, but the man with the sandy hair would have none of it. He raised his baton with a threatening air, saying: "No, or it will be death or life." He meant that if they owned up to their involvement, they were sure to be sentenced to death by hanging or a life sentence.

The officers then went to the spot where Broadfoot had fallen in. There was a discernible ripple in the water a short distance from the bank. "Nobody saw the boy go in," said the man with the sandy whiskers. He became even more insistent that they tell no one, warning his colleague that if the affair was ever reported it would be equally bad for them both because they had both been there at the kilns. The pair returned to their beat.

Now that the coast was clear for Wilson, he went back onto the kilns where he found Campbell hiding. Campbell had heard the splash too. They discussed the incident and decided that Broadfoot had likely found his own way out and must be hunkering down somewhere in the complex of buildings. Since there was not much they could do to find him in the dark, they tried to catch up on some sleep. When first light dawned the next morning, Broadfoot still hadn't appeared. The young men looked around the works for him, searching everywhere, but finding no sign. Their alarm was growing—it looked as though he had not got out of the water after all. They broke cover and approached a kiln worker, James McCluskey, to tell him what they had seen the night before. At first he didn't believe them. "It can't be possible," he said, but Wilson replied: "As sure as the water's there, he's in it." When Hunter came forward and corroborated this, McCluskey began to think there could be some truth in the story. He accompanied them to the spot and marked an X on the path. He obtained grappling irons and for two hours searched the basin, but found nothing. In the early morning of Saturday, the three boys formed a party with McCluskey and other kiln workers to search the canal once again. A third search on Sunday revealed no trace. Because of the possibility of being classed as vagrants, the boys discouraged the employees of Watson and Son from approaching the police.

On Sunday afternoon, however, Wilson relented. He stopped Constable Thomas Boomer on the street and told him what had happened. Like McCluskey, Boomer was sceptical at first, but took Hunter, Campbell and Wilson to the northern police office. His senior officer, Lieutenant Daniel Taylor, could scarcely believe the story. He kept the boys in custody while he waited for the two policemen concerned, Robert Sinclair and Roderick McLaughlin, to return from their beat. When they got back, Taylor questioned them and they admitted to having chased some youths away from the spot. McLaughlin said it wasn't true that one had ended up in the water. While this questioning was going on the sandy-whiskered officer Sinclair appeared to be overtaken by a kind of temporary paralysis. Once he regained his composure, he denied it. The superintendent gave instructions to his officers to investigate.

On Monday morning Wilson accompanied day-inspector William Smith to the basin, and pointed out where the incident had happened.

The canal was thoroughly dragged and in deep water at the east end of the basin, something was found jammed between pieces of wood. It was the body of John Broadfoot in his once-white clothing. Back at Maitland Street Wilson identified the deceased. The police surgeon, Dr Robert Renfrew, carried out a thorough examination and reported that the limbs were flaccid and the hair matted with wet mud, while the face had a dark, leaden look. He could find no disease present that could account for the death. There was no evidence of violence and the signs were consistent with drowning.

At first both officers were held in prison while the matter was investigated. However, it became clear that McLaughlin had wanted to report the incident but had been intimidated into keeping silent. Sinclair alone was tried before a crowded court, entering a not guilty plea. He consistently denied having assaulted one of the boys, causing him to tumble into the canal and ultimately to drown. The witnesses included Broadfoot's homeless companions, his mother Mary Ann, two physicians and furnace worker McLuskey.

Addressing the jury, the advocate depute declared that there could be no doubt that Broadfoot had drowned, so the question was whether he had met his death by accident or as a result of the prisoner's actions. Though the witnesses were young men of low social status, they had stuck to their story consistently and appeared very earnest that their friend's death should be investigated. Dr Watson, speaking for the prisoner, said that only one person had seen the act, and the likelihood was that Broadfoot had slipped. However, the jury did not accept this. After only a few minutes they returned the verdict of guilty of culpable homicide and Sinclair was sentenced to 10 years of penal servitude.

The phenomenon of homeless people sleeping rough at canalside kilns would go on throughout the industrial period and was still occurring well into the twentieth century. In the November of that month, eleven men were rounded up by police after reports were received of them sheltering beside the warmth of the chambers at Blackwell Brickworks, Cadder, close to the Forth and Clyde. The men, described as probably of no fixed abode, were taken to

Bishopbriggs Police Station. Instead of trying to address the problem of the men's homelessness, the matter was dealt with through the J P Court, where they were admonished. It was treated as a crime because they hadn't got permission to be there from the proprietor of the works. The same approach was taken in 1936, when seven "vagrants", the majority of Irish extraction, were charged with having lodged in brick kilns at Callendar Coal Company Brickworks and at Roughcastle without consent. Four of the men, who expressed regret at what they had done, were admonished. The others, being repeat offenders, were given short prison sentences, two of twenty-one days and the other to ten days in prison. One of the repeat offenders, Charles McGinty, ably articulated the circular situation in which he found himself. He had suffered eight years of poverty and misery and was perfectly willing to work if only a job could be found. "I have nowhere to go, sir," he told Sheriff-Substitute Nimmo at Falkirk Sheriff Court, "I have to sleep somewhere." He added that when he came out of Saughton Prison he would end up having to sleep in the kilns or a similar place again, since he would receive no public assistance money from the Labour Exchange at Falkirk.

Perhaps the hardships of the world wars helped to bring about a wider understanding of the causes of kiln-sleeping in some circles, but the authorities continued to view it as an offence. In October 1950, three boys were charged with stealing potatoes and a report in the *Daily Mail* headed "Melancholy Picture of Poverty" highlighted the well-known fact that between thirty and fifty unemployed people slept at brick kilns in the Glasgow area. Their existence was a communal one, since it involved stealing food during the day, which was then cooked at the kilns and distributed among the group. One of the three had found himself with nowhere to sleep after losing both his parents. He had been admonished after a previous rough-sleeping offence and sent back to his native town of Kilmarnock, but as there was no one there who would help him, he had ended up back at the kilns. Another pair described how their travels to find work had been unsuccessful. The *Daily Mail* report recommended that the public money used for administering punishments would be better spent addressing the boys' plight and issued a plea to authority figures to do something about it. The Justice, Mr Kaye of Millbrae, expressed his hope that the three lads would obtain employment but this would be scant comfort, since he nonetheless sent them to the Bridewell, a house of correction for petty offenders.

The Gingerbread Seller

By Bridge 49 at Causewayend on the Union Canal, a woman's body was found following a frenzied attack that had stripped away her dignity. Most of her garments had been removed, stabs and cuts disfigured her face and body and her head was almost severed from her neck. Her bloodstained clothing, a shoe and an empty money-pocket were found within 200 yards. The woman was known to be Euphemia Bourhill, a fifty-year-old pedlar who had been missing for nearly a month. The surgeon who carried out the post mortem took the view that Bourhill had been left in the water for anything between ten and twenty days. Stating the obvious, he said there could be no doubt that it had been a case of murder, with the weapon most likely a large-bladed knife. It appeared that her clothing had been removed in order to wipe up blood at the scene. The last sighting of Bourhill had been at midnight on 15th October, 1847, as she made her way back to the outskirts of Edinburgh from the Mid Calder Fair. Bourhill's lot had not been an easy one. She had lived an insecure life of travelling the country from one fair or market to another selling gingerbread and fruit.

Had a woman from the genteel classes gone missing, then been discovered in the Union Canal following savage murderous attack, a widespread sensation would surely have blown up. Presumably Bourhill's itinerant lifestyle explains the absence of a public appeal following her disappearance, and her lowly status could explain why the press saw fit to give a few meagre paragraphs to the incident. In any case, it appeared that the mystery would be cleared up within days. Within days a Mr Lang, whose first name is not recorded, was apprehended for questioning. Like her, he was a gingerbread seller who had been making his way home to Edinburgh from the fair. He was seen in Bourhill's company, or at least in her vicinity, at the time of the last sighting. The circumstantial evidence against him appeared overwhelming. He had blood on his coat and an obvious wound to his eye.

In custody Lang was not forthcoming at to Bourhill's last hours. However, it is possible to piece together a general impression of the twice-yearly fair they had both attended. It had been business as usual in that crowds from Edinburgh, Glasgow and the country districts had descended on the area—farmers, horse and cattle dealers, farm servants seeking work, travelling musicians, people looking for a day's entertainment, and the inevitable pickpockets—yet proceedings were subdued. The potato disease that was devastating Ireland also blighted crops in the Scottish Highlands and this seemed to have a depressive effect on agricultural activity. More farm servants than ever sought employment; many left without work, or had to accept wages considerably lower than the previous year's. Roadster horses, the nineteenth century equivalent of an about-town car, were up for sale, but these beasts were of poor quality. Of the 400 cattle available, few were bought. The only success was a show of work horses which moved a Mr Edgeley of Gilmerton to pay £100 for his favourite. High jinks at the fair were quelled by a large detachment of watching police officers, led by a Superintendent List. They had been tipped off that labourers working on the Caledonian Railway had just been paid, a situation that might lead to riotous behaviour breaking out. This came to nought.

As for Bourhill, she was known to have left the fair with a modest 20 shillings from her day's work in her pocket. Rumour had it that Lang had become drunk and irritable at the fair, that he had been seen arguing fiercely with Bourhill and hadn't got home until 8 o'clock the following morning. The man could not account for the wound to his eye but lacking firm evidence, the police had to set him free. Questions were left hanging as to the woman's final movements. Ten days after the gruesome find the authorities put up a reward of £50 for information that could be passed to the procurator fiscal. The information being sought was very specific. The authorities believed the unfortunate woman had met her end on the road to Edinburgh between Kiershill and Hermiston and they wanted to understand how her body could have been moved to the Union Canal. A number of theories were offered in the press, but ultimately no one came forward with the answer. As the months wore on her sad demise faded from memory.

An unexpected development happened two years later. Word was spreading that an eighteen-year-old who worked as a canal horse driver knew something about the incident. This caused a stir as he was implicating a trio of boatmen connected with the Union Canal— two of whom were notorious as far as the police were concerned. Presumably for his own protection, the man's identity was kept secret, and the procurator fiscal had him brought to Edinburgh for questioning about what he knew. He claimed to have first-hand knowledge of the incident, saying that on the night of the murder he had been driving a boat with three crew members aboard who also worked as carters—James Gray of Edinburgh, known as Earl Grey, Mungo Duff from Ratho and James Turnbull of Linlithgow. On the night of 15th October 1847, a woman fitting the description of Bourhill had boarded at Hermiston. She was travelling west. Since the tow ropes were long the driver was working a distance away from the boat and didn't see what went on during the next part of the journey; that must have been when the attack happened. His next sight of the boat disturbed him deeply. Bourhill lay outstretched on the bottom clearly dead, her face and body mutilated horribly. Her clothes had been removed, apparently having been used as rags to mop up the blood. The driver was warned by the trio that if he breathed a word to anyone, he would meet a similarly grisly end. Out of the twenty shillings the assailants had stolen from their victim the lad was offered one shilling, a promised bribe that he said was never honoured. The macabre voyage went on and near Causewayend the body was pushed off the side into the water.

The driver claimed he hadn't come forward at first as he had been too afraid, but now the ringleader, Earl Grey, was in jail on a separate charge of theft. After the driver came forward, Turnbull was apprehended at Linlithgow and Duff at Ratho in connection with the murder and thorough investigations were put in train; yet after that, the records fall silent. It seems that the young driver's word against three men would not be enough. In some respects his story checked out, such as the fact that she boarded at Hermiston, but it didn't make sense that she was travelling west—away from her home. A writer for the the *Falkirk Herald* was sceptical about the driver's claims, suggesting he was up to no good. One plausible turn of events is that Lang killed her and then enlisted the three boatmen to shift the evidence into the water; they were, after all, also carters. Whoever the guilty party was, they had wrongly supposed that the remains of Euphemia Bourhill would sink without trace. That is a mistake that many a canal offender has made.

The Tin Box

January 20th 1883 was a Saturday evening like any other in Glasgow. The foundries and manufactories lining the Forth and Clyde Canal had closed their gates at the usual time of 6 o'clock. The Tradeston Gasworks, with its sprawling buildings and four gas holders close to Lilybank Road, had sent all of its employees home with the exception of a gas inspector and the manager. Railway passenger services were running as normal, although workers were stretched because some drivers and points men had gone on strike to protest at having to work long hours without any break. People were out walking, warming themselves in public houses and milling around shops, some of which would stay open much later than we would expect today. The only sign that something unusual might be about to happen was the presence of a few strangers on the streets that night. So far they had gone largely unnoticed.

Foundry worker George Murray lived with his wife on Wigton Street, close to the aqueduct taking the canal across Possil Road. The couple had a few drinks at home in the evening and at 11pm they left to head south along Garscube Road. Close to Dobbie's

Loan, they parted company and George went into a urinal. At the entrance, he stumbled against two men coming out who were lugging a container—a large tin box that was apparently very heavy, as it took the two of them to hold it. Murray glanced at the box and wondered what on earth could be in it. It was the kind of container women often used to keep their bonnets in and appeared to be in pristine condition.

As Murray stumbled against them, one of the men uttered a grumpy exclamation and accused him of being clumsy. He was the taller of the two and wore a short brown coat. There was an air of threat in his voice that set Murray on edge. Murray thought the man's anger was out of proportion, so he retorted, "Surely you must have eggs in your box, you're so much afraid… " A short argument then ensued, though fortunately it petered out before matters could escalate. The whereabouts of the tin box would be unknown for a further two hours.

Elsewhere in the city the Barr brothers, Adam, Archibald and Matthew, had been out visiting with four of their friends. Adam was a gunner with the Royal Artillery. Twenty-three years of age, he was on leave from his regiment in Coventry to visit his native Springburn. At one o'clock the group wound up their night out and made to return home by the canal towpath. As they reached the Possil Road aqueduct, they slowed down. They had spotted an object glinting in the moonlight. Close to the water someone had left a large tin box, oval in shape, and apparently fastened with a clasp or padlock. At this sight one of the women in the company became uneasy. Canal bridges were notoriously a place for desperate women to abandon their babies. It was decided that they should investigate, in case an infant might be trapped inside.

Nearest the box was Gunner Barr. As he bent down he saw that the clasp hadn't actually been secured. He lifted the lid. Inside was a light-coloured material that might be sand or sawdust. He put his hand in and began to root about. In the act of doing so, he triggered an alarming blur of events that the group of friends would later struggle to recount to the police. It started with a bang like gunpowder going off. Then a vivid blue flame sparked out of the tin box and leapt high into the air. Sound fizzed about their ears and the box began to give of a strange, distinctive smell that carried over the water and drifted along the canal path. Adam Barr was horror-struck. Although rooted to the spot, he managed to call out to the others to flee.

"You've shot me!" one of the brothers exclaimed amid the confusion. Everyone had been blown back by the force of blast. Adam Barr, who was bleeding slightly, had just resolved to set off to find a policeman when there followed a second, louder explosion, which blew the lid clean off the box. He looked down. He'd sustained burns and cuts to his left hand and arm, his face had been hit by flying debris, and some of the others had minor injuries. For about fifteen minutes they stood watching the box from a distance, until the fizzing ceased. At last they judged it safe to approach, and found the container to be now nearly empty of the mystery substance. The artillery man was puzzled as to what it could be. He had plenty of experience of gunpowder and nitro-cellulose, but the persistent smell indicated it was neither of these.

Two night constables, Joseph Anderson and Thomas Frater, had been out separately on patrol nearby when they heard the explosion coming from the direction of the aqueduct. Heading towards it, they encountered the shaken young people. Constable Anderson removed the box and led the group to the Northern Police Office to have their wounds cleaned and dressed by the police surgeon. Meanwhile, Frater sought a senior officer, then returned to the bridge with Inspector Donald Ferguson. Close to an area of blackened ground they found traces of something that looked like sawdust. Searching the scene, Frater found a brass tube and Ferguson found a brass cap, which turned out to fit perfectly together. Although there had been injuries, the explosion could have been considerably worse. If the aqueduct had been damaged to the point of collapse, a deluge of canal water would have been released onto the streets below, threatening lives, flooding city dwellers out of their homes and putting a stop to boat navigation.

Unknown to the Barr brothers and their friends, this was the third explosion of the evening in the city. The first, and largest, had occurred just after ten o'clock at Tradeston Gasworks. The southern sky had been lit by a bright, leaping flame that appeared to come from holder No. 4, which stood on its own within walls to the south of Lilybank Road. In the seconds that followed a sound stammered out like gunshots, followed by rumbling that went on for some minutes. Houses shook, windows were shattered and a row of cottages partly collapsed. A woman holding a baby was found dazed in the street, having jumped out of a window. Eleven residents of the collapsed cottages, some of them children, were taken to the infirmary suffering from burns to the face and hands.

Flames licked around gas holder No. 4 until it collapsed. The hundreds of householders who poured onto the streets circulated the theory that there had been an escape of gas that caught light from a flame. The fire brigade were on the scene within minutes and quickly ascertained this as the source of the catastrophe. Discussions went on with gasworks staff and it was agreed that the safest course of action would be to allow the blaze to burn itself out. The investigations were brought to halt when suddenly the area was plunged into darkness. Power was soon restored.

The second explosion had occurred in the north of the city. A report rang out in the darkness, stirring fears that a shoot-out had erupted at the Maryhill barracks. But in the minutes that followed, the blast was traced to a Caledonian Railway bridge crossing Dobbie's Loan, a short way from Buchanan Street passenger station. Flames had shot across the line, the doors of a rail shed blew wide open and its brickwork was destroyed. A number of employees, including a driver, managed to dive out of reach of the flying bricks and debris. For years the shed had been used for the coaling and watering of engines. By sheer good luck, it had been replaced and taken out of use only weeks before by the railway company.

As news spread that there had been three explosions at separate sites, general anxiety grew and the authorities were on alert. Sentries were posted at aqueducts and railway stations and the gasworks was closely guarded. Newspapers throughout the country devoted pages to the dramatic events, with a consensus emerging that the incidents must have been planned with malicious intent. But who could have been responsible for such a thing? One school of thought turned to the Caledonian Railway workers' strike. Only days before, a sizeable group of engine drivers and pointsmen had voted to express their discontent at having to work anything up to twelve hours without a break, and other workers had been brought in to keep the trains running. It was asked whether this could be more than a coincidence. Was there bad blood between the two groups of railway workers?

In the following days, experts were ushered in to inspect the three explosion sites. A representative of the Nobel explosives company examined the tin box from the aqueduct and declared categorically that the sand-like substance was not dynamite. An eminent gas engineer, Thomas Hawksley, was summoned. He abandoned all his business in London and travelled up by night mail. He concluded that the gasworks incident hadn't resulted from a flow of gas escaping and igniting, but from a substance purposely placed outside the cylinder. Next in line to investigate was an explosives specialist named Colonel Vivian Dering Majendie, who was commissioned to carry out a thorough investigation of all three sites. In mid-February the Colonel came back with the surprising news that the substance at the aqueduct was a nitro compound that had never been licensed for use in the country.

Police investigations continued. A fuse they had found near the gasworks added to the overall impression of foul play. The disgruntled railwaymen theory was now being discounted. The authorities noted that there were good grounds for connecting the Glasgow incidents with goings-on south of the border. Two years previously there had been a bomb blast at a barracks in Salford. A few months later, explosives were found concealed on board two boats at Liverpool. Notable people had received threatening letters, in recent weeks there here had been an attempt to destroy the office of the *Times* newspaper, and a secret nitro-glycerine manufacturing operation had been raided in Birmingham. Fingers pointed to shadowy Irish nationalist societies, which were suspected to have representatives in

Glasgow. In Ireland, nationalist plots were high in the population's consciousness, not least the murders of two British government administrators in Phoenix Park the previous year. In early 1883, a network of suspects had been arrested in Dublin and charged with conspiracy to murder.

In Glasgow, speculation gradually died down, until a decisive development took place on the evening of Friday, 6th April. Police Superintendent John Boyd stationed himself in Garscube Road, close to Dobbie's Loan. Boyd was acting on information that the man he wanted, an Irishman, would be passing this way en route to a pub. He watched and waited; and when the figure did appear, Boyd had no difficulty in picking him out from the crowd. He was in his early 30s, tall and broad-shouldered, and dressed in a soft felt hat and other clothing that indicated he had recently been in America. His behaviour was practically a parody of a suspicious man: his hat was drawn down to hide his face and he glanced all around him furtively. He was perhaps already a little drunk. Boyd went in pursuit. No sooner had the man got inside the pub than a posse of officers stepped forward and collared him.

At the Central Police Office, the man gave his name in an Irish-American accent as Bernard Gallagher. He had lived for five years in Maryhill, working at the time in the Firhill Foundry. After that he had been absent in America and Liverpool. On his return to Glasgow he was known for always having plenty of money despite his apparently idle status. On the Saturday morning following Gallagher's arrest, officers charged him with having been involved in the explosions at Tradeston and Possil Bridge. Smiling and unconcerned, the accused claimed he had been in America at the time of the offences. He could prove that he had left America for this country with his brother and another man on 8th February. Despite police discretion about the arrest, the newspapers were quick to pick up that his brother was one Dr Thomas Gallagher from Brooklyn. He had recently been taken up by police in London in connection with explosions south of the border, along with four other men.

The Gallagher brothers quickly became notorious figures and

newspaper reporters set about trying to find out what they could about their past. They had been born in Scotland of Irish parentage. Dr Thomas was said to be 'a humane physician' with a long patient list. Intriguingly it became known that chemistry was his special area of expertise, fuelling speculation that he might be well-informed as to the composition and use of explosives. His brother Bernard was removed from Glasgow to London to be questioned with the others. At the trial in June 1883, Bernard Gallagher's legal representative argued that his chief interest in life was drinking. In general he was to be found in a condition a long way short of sober that would make him a most unlikely conspirator. The money he was noted for possessing had been sent to him out of kindness by his more stable brother. Two women claimed to have seen Bernard behaving strangely close to the Glasgow gasometer but his involvement could not be proved beyond doubt. The jury took less than an hour and a half to acquit Bernard and one of the other accused men. Dr Thomas Gallagher remained infamous and was seen as the ringleader and brains of the operation. He and three others were found guilty and given the unenviable sentence of penal servitude for life. In the courtroom, the brothers were seen to exchange a heartfelt goodbye.

While the three Glasgow atrocities faded from the public gaze, the police sustained their investigations in the background. On 1st September, 1883, they arrested another six men on a charge of laying down the tin box with intent to destroy the aqueduct, and causing the other two explosions. Two of them were chemical workers and all were believed to be members of a 'Ribbon Society'. Security was high and at the trial the public was kept out. The prosecution said that the men had hatched the conspiracy in America and had made use of an explosives factory in Birmingham, which was hidden under the pretext of being a paint-mixing business.

Among the productions were the tin box found by Gunner Barr at the aqueduct, a brass tube, a sample of lignin dynamite and an envelope addressed to J Montgomery & Co, manufacturing chemists, Port Dundas, Glasgow, containing a receipt for the preparation of explosives. Evidence was provided by Colonel Majendie that he had seen the same substance seized on the two boats in Liverpool in 1881, and believed it to be connected with the Irish activists. The case rested heavily on the testimony of one George Hughes, who had belonged to the ribbon society but maintained he didn't participate in the conspiracy.

George Murray, who had bumped into the men clutching the tin box, was called as a witness and asked to recall the uneasy encounter. He and other witnesses who saw the strangers in the city that night found it difficult to make definitive identifications. The judge stated that it could be proved in three cases that the men were in the vicinity of the gasholder shortly before the explosions, and he didn't doubt that the others were their confederates. All were found guilty of intending to destroy or seriously damage people and property and sentenced to penal servitude, five of them for life. Those sentenced to only seven years were believed to have been unaware of the full extent of the conspiracy. Superintendent Boyd was one of three officers given a medal for aiding the men's capture.

The prisoners were taken under armed guard to serve their sentences south of the border. Regarded as particularly dangerous individuals, they were singled out to be kept in grim conditions, fed on burnt bread and dishwater, and punished severely if they were seen even looking at one another. Three of the men were issued a release date in December 1890, although one of them succumbed to the dreadful conditions and died of TB and depression shortly before. Dr Thomas Gallagher was said to have become insane owing to the strictures of his confinement and left for American on his release in 1896. Whether his brother went with him is not recorded.

A Ticket-of-Leave Man

It was the summer of 1861. Just before 9 o'clock in the morning the coal scow Alexander set off on its regular return journey from Townhead to Coatbridge. In charge of the vessel was twenty-one-year-old Matthew Cross. Looking up at Robertson's Bridge, Cross spotted a man standing there and recognised him as fellow boatman

William Roughead, better known as Rough Will. Rough Will was the last man anyone would want to see. Rumours were sweeping the canal that on the previous evening he had stabbed a Glasgow man and left him seriously wounded—he was now on the run. As the boat drew near to the bridge, everything happened quickly. Rough Will stepped forward to the edge and launched himself aboard the Alexander, saying "For God's sake let me to the hind end, oot the sicht", meaning he wanted to get himself out of sight. He quickly made his way down into the cabin and threw himself onto a bed. In a state of extreme agitation and shifting between sitting and lying, he muttered to himself about the awful situation he had got himself into. Cross had never seen anyone in such a state.

Asked what was wrong, Rough Will mumbled about having been in a fuddle often before, and he doubted if this would be the "hindmost" of it. Cross asked if the rumour about the stabbing was true. Rough Will didn't answer directly, but claimed five or six men had sprung at him out of a close and set on him. Cross didn't believe him. It was clear that Will was fleeing as a result of some deed he had committed. He asked Rough Will more questions and got him to admit that he had thrown his boatman's knife into a cornfield and was planning to go east to his father's house to get clothes and money. From there he would proceed to England. Boatman Cross deduced, though he didn't dare mention it, that the police would be looking for him.

In Glasgow the detective force had swung into action within minutes of the attack on the city's Garngad Road. Superintendent McCall of central district had mustered his men with instructions that this ruffian must be caught, and they began to gather information from locals about the attacker's movements. Sergeant Andrew McBroom and Constable William Harley, who knew Rough Will well for all the wrong reasons, got a tip-off that he had been on the canal bank in the Townhead area just before a scow had been seen setting off in the direction of Coatbridge. It was a reasonable assumption that the fugitive would be hiding out on board. The two officers exchanged their uniforms for plain clothes and set off along the canal in pursuit of the Alexander. Rough Will and Matthew Cross both worked on the scows that went between Glasgow and Grangemouth, but that was all they had in common. The Cross family led a settled life at their home in Dundyvan Road in Coatbridge and father and son, both called Matthew, operated the Alexander on behalf of a Wishaw coal company. This was a far cry from Rough Will's circumstances. At forty years of age, he had no fixed abode and was in the habit of settling down for the night on a boat in the Port Dundas area. From time to time he managed to pay for a bed at a lodging house in the city's Milton Street. His financial situation was not helped by a long-running drink problem which had got him into trouble on many occasions and was testing the patience of his employer, Charles Mooney. Originally a native of County Armagh, Mooney owned several scows that plied the Monkland Canal and ran two spirit dealing outlets in Glasgow, one at Castle Street and a larger premises next door to his house at 153 Garngad Road. Mooney, who was sixty years old, had lost his wife and son within the last three years and the debts that would put him out of business in 1863 were probably already beginning to mount up. Mooney had warned Rough Will about not getting into any more of his "fuddles". Will had the tendency to be easily antagonised when he had been drinking; moreover, a chilling incident back in 1849 had shown that he was capable of calculated violence.

On a September evening that year, Mary McCue and Robert Hutton had been strolling along Falkirk's High Street towards the Cross Keys Inn. As they drew level with a close mouth, Will Roughead and another man dashed out and seized Hutton, only to deal him a savage blow with a beer bottle, which broke and sent Hutton reeling to the ground. The terrified McCue ran off to get help while the attackers aimed one kick after another to their victim's head, then rifled in his waistcoat pocket for their prize of three half crowns, seven shillings and sixpence, a tobacco box and a ginger beer bottle. Although blood was flowing in quantity from his nose, Hutton tried to put up a fight by getting hold of Roughead's leg and refusing to let it go. At this point, Roughead shouted "come and give him a kick," on which cry a third man appeared from the close mouth and piled into the assault. When the help summoned by Mary McCue arrived, the men were chased away and later apprehended. At the trial, which took place the following April, it emerged that one of the men, Benjamin 'Haggart' Nicol had notched up three previous convictions. By a large majority the trio was found guilty and sentenced to 15 years transportation across the seas.

On the other side of the world Rough Will must have conducted himself well enough as he was given a ticket-of-leave in 1856. The ticket-of-leave was a remission of sentence, and bestowed privileges such as the right to bring family members to Australia or to earn money. However, they were often restrictions such as a ban on gun ownership or an order not to leave the vicinity of the colony. The ticket-of-leave system was controversial in some quarters, with newspapers carrying heavily critical reports of criminal deeds done by returned convicts while on a ticket-of-leave.

By some means William Roughead had managed to procure passage on a boat and was back in Scotland in the late 1850s. Charles Mooney was giving Rough Will a second chance by employing him, but in the end the boatman's unruly behaviour during the course of several years proved too much. On that fateful evening in July in 1861, Mooney confronted him in the Garngad Road premises and sacked him, telling him that he had a chance of getting his job back only if he would give up drinking. In the twenty-four hours that followed, Rough Will visited Mooney's public house no less than four times. During the first visit he asked for the loan of a shilling, and when this was refused he said he would content himself with a sixpence, or a gill of whisky. Rough Will left the shop empty-handed. On the second visit, Mooney asked Rough Will to take a jar of whisky to his other premises in Castle Street. Miraculously, this instruction was carried out without incident. The next visit, however, was a different matter. It was between nine and ten in the evening, the hour when the night police came on duty, and Rough Will arrived looking distinctly tipsy and quarrelsome, and took a seat at the end of the counter. He was escorted to the doorstep by the irritated Mooney, but would go no further and, to the annoyance of people in the shop, paced up and down while muttering angrily about his dismissal. He remarked that it was "a damned shame that a man who had been driving boats all the year should be humbugged by an old bugger like Mooney." Mooney sent out his assistant to summon the police. Two men from the night patrol arrived and ushered him away.

It was perhaps inevitable that Rough Will would come back within the half hour. A struggle ensued to eject him from the premises, during which Mooney grabbed a stick and struck Will on the face. The dust-up was observed by two young men, Bernard Bryceland and Tom McDonald. Bryceland was a twenty-seven-year-old furnace worker. Once the troublemaker was gone, Bryceland had a conversation with McDonald about it, then left to return to his wife and baby further along the road. He exited by the side door, which gave onto a passageway that led to several dwellings including Mooney's. It was here that he bumped into Rough Will. It appeared Will had paid a short-lived visit to the house of Peggy Devine, widow of a boatman. There was blood on his left cheek where Mooney had struck him.

The furnace worker took him by the shoulder and advised him to go home to get the blood washed off his face. Roughead said nothing and made to walk away, but was so drunk that he staggered against Peggy Devine's window. The other man turned back and caught hold of him, placing him against the wall just beyond the window and made to go away. The inebriated man shouted: "Here, here, come back!" Bryceland again advised him to go home and it was in that moment, when a hand swiftly moved towards his face, that the world became a blur for Bryceland. Though he didn't actually see the knife, he knew he had been stabbed in the neck. He threw up his arm, knocking his attacker back and in a sort of daze ran through the close. He did not yet realise the extent of his injury.

With Roughead's shouts of "Come on, you bugger!" ringing in his ears, Bryceland stumbled onto Garngad Road and met Malcolm McIntyre, night sergeant of the central district police. McIntyre saw that his clothes were saturated with blood. He sent a constable for a local medic and had the distressed man taken to his father-in-law's house. Bryceland managed to say that he had been stabbed by a man who'd been causing trouble at Mooney's—a man he would recognise, though he didn't know his name. Moments later Dr John McQuat had arrived. Alarmed by the seriousness of the haemorrhage, McQuat sent for further medical expertise and applied basic treatment. The wound penetrated more than two inches in length. The weapon, he thought, had been inserted with great force and turned before it was withdrawn. No less than four medical men arrived, with police surgeon McGill the most senior. McGill put a stitch in the wound, but this did little to help, and a teaspoonful of whisky and water only caused water to gush from the patient's mouth. The immense quantity of blood suggested that the knife had gone through to the gullet. Bryceland was slipping towards death, his pulse faint, his eyesight failing and his face turning white. McGill decided that only radical intervention could save him, and time was of the essence. The only option, he thought, was to tie the carotid artery, the main blood vessel of the neck. This carried considerable risk, as the procedure had seldom been attempted before. McGill carried it out with the support of the other medics and by this means stopped the haemorrhage and saved the young man's life.

During the course of that night and the next morning, the police continued to comb Garngad Road and the canal area for Rough Will. Sergeant McBroom and Constable Harley caught up with the Alexander when it was about five miles from Glasgow. McBroom asked whether Rough Will was aboard and Matthew Cross, realising that these were policemen, said that he was. The officers found their quarry in the hold. Lamenting, "This will do me no good, after what I got before," Rough Will was detained and charged with stabbing Bryceland in the neck, thus endangering his life. The furnace worker had been left exhausted by the attack and had difficulty explaining to the police what had happened. A week afterwards he was able to go for a short walk on Garngad Road but still blood seeped from the wound several times. Dr McGill issued a report in late September. There would probably be little further loss of blood, he said, but it would be "highly improper and dangerous" for Bryceland to appear at the trial then scheduled for 1st November. The date was revised. On the 12^{th,} McGill reported that the young man would now be well enough to appear in the court at the end of the month.

Rough Will pled not guilty and claimed he acted in self-defence, but several witnesses in and around Mooney's public house could attest to his inebriated, quarrelsome state. Dr McGill described the severity of the wound and the immediate threat to Bryceland's life. Rough Will's attempt to flee was described in eloquent detail by the young Matthew Cross. The prisoner was found guilty. The judge, Lord Ardmillan, declared he had narrowly escaped execution, and that he could not sentence him to less than penal servitude for life. For the second time in his life, Will was transported to a prison hulk, and in 1863 he was one of 270 convicts setting sail for Western Australia on the Lord Dalhousie. Given his past history it was unlikely that he would be granted a ticket-of-leave a second time. In its report on the trial, The *Glasgow Herald* praised the actions of McGill and his assistants as "an example of the triumph of surgery in saving human life from the brink of the grave."

Combinations

After four years of excavation and many a setback, the Union Canal was finished and opened to boats in May 1822. A few lesser jobs remained to be done, such as the building of stables for company horses along the route and the creation of a water feeder system high in the Pentlands at Cobbinshaw. Some former Union Canal navvies got work on the boats, not least William Hare who later found international notoriety with his partner-in-murder, William Burke. In 1822 Hare was a lumper at the basin, Port Hopetoun, loading coals for the biggest merchant James Dawson, agent for the Duke of Hamilton. Other former navvies were not so lucky. In 1825, scores of former Union Canal labourers still haunted the decaying rabbit warrens of Edinburgh's Old Town and surrounding areas, and spent their time trying to procure employment and finding a decent place to live. These men had to be prepared to get on the move and work in any capacity, wherever they could. In the autumn, those seeking agricultural work poured into the Grassmarket for the hiring fair. This was a time when the labouring classes were in a particularly difficult position. Reapers, shearers, shipwrights, paper-makers and the operators of machines had all formed combination, an early form of trades union, and gone on strike. Ill-tempered scuffles had broken out among workers in Stirlingshire, Falkirk, Glasgow and Edinburgh. The legal position of the combinations was unclear. Laws banning them for a quarter of a century had recently been relaxed, leading to vexed parliamentary debates on how to deal with them. Some argued that not only could the combinations spark stoppages of labour, but their very existence posed a danger. They could whip up a fury and lead to breaches of the peace; even, as one outraged commentator claimed, drive the discontented to murder. On the other hand, it was widely recognised that many powerful industrial magnates were getting away with shocking exploitation. Some were known to conspire to depress wages, with a few unscrupulous enough to starve their employees into submission.

One such combination came together in the Wester Portsburgh district of Edinburgh, and its members included Irishmen who had dug the canal. Perhaps feelings were already running high among them when a farm servant named Alexander Thain arrived at the hiring fair looking for prospective sheep shearers. Thain had been sent by his master from Ravelrig, to the south-west of Edinburgh. He wasn't long in securing a few labourers at the price of two shillings and sixpence. As they began to clamber into his farm cart, Thain felt increasingly uneasy. A group of Irishmen stood watching him carefully. They were strapping young men with a surly attitude. Once all the prospective shearers were seated in the cart, Thain climbed into the driving seat and got ready to take them to their new place of work. The wheels no sooner began to turn than the Irishmen from the combination stepped forward and surrounded the cart so that it couldn't move. They had a point to make, and they made it forcibly. No labourer was to leave, they said, who had been engaged for less than one pound a week, or three shillings and four pence per day with victuals provided. They grew increasingly angry and began to manhandle the cart, shaking it violently till it overturned. One of their number appeared to be particularly enraged. The terrified shearers fled but Thain was not so lucky. The angry man grabbed him by the collar and gave him a sound beating.

Fortunately for the farm servant, his assailant was quickly overpowered and taken directly to the nearest police office, where the magistrate was sitting. He identified himself as John Fox, boatman for the merchant James Dawson. Thain related what had happened and justice was dispensed on the spot: Fox was fined ten shillings and sixpence, a sum that was paid by one of his associates. The combination then made its way back to the Grassmarket, where they could be gratified by the result of their efforts: the price of hiring had in the majority of cases gone up to two shillings a day. Nevertheless, they were still seen as a threat. By midday the Grassmarket was swarming with police. Thain decided to steer clear of the site of the trouble. In the early afternoon he headed towards the canal basin. As he proceeded along the road, though, he began to realise that he was not alone. Justice had done nothing to deter his assailant; perhaps it had only inflamed the situation, for a furious-looking John Fox was coming in pursuit. Thain stepped up his pace, then saw with some relief that the Irishman had disappeared into a house in Wester Portsburgh.

But any relief would only be temporary. Moments later, Fox emerged from the house clutching a cudgel. The alarmed Thain crossed Lothian Road to the south eastern entrance of the canal basin—which happened to be Fox's place of work. Fox came up behind him and struck a vicious blow to his right ear. Thain was brought down to the ground, helpless and insensible, and suffered a further blow to his brow. This was all witnessed by Alexander Hook, another farm servant who had seen the original incident in the Grassmarket. Hook pursued Fox in through the gate to the canal basin, but Fox must have escaped through the other side. Meanwhile, the dazed Thain was carried to the shop of Peter Mitchell Hill, a surgeon who had premises at Downie Place. A second medic, Dr Adam Messer, called in and confirmed that Thain was in a sorry state. Two neighbours of his who were in the district for the hiring fair took him back to Ravelrig by cart, one man holding his head all the way. Back at Ravelrig, the patient was seen by surgeon William Newbigging, who signed a report saying that his life was in danger owing to a blow from a bludgeon. It would be the best part of the week until favourable symptoms began to appear. Two weeks after the attack he managed to get out of bed and it was a further two weeks before he could begin to do simple work tasks. However, in the long term he had been left with frequent dizzy spells.

Although Fox stayed away from his place of work, he was found and held in prison for four months before the matter came to trial. His colleagues, James MacPherson and Roderick Fraser, gave testimony that they'd never known him to be in trouble before and his employer, James Dawson, supported Fox, saying that he was a quiet and well-behaved character who didn't engage in quarrels. Unmoved by this, the jury found him guilty within a few minutes. The sheriff sentenced him to six months in the Bridewell, the house of correction within the prison on Calton Hill. As for the combination, its activities would soon be cut short. With trouble spreading across districts throughout the United Kingdom, Parliament approved new legislation clamping down on the associations.

A Christmas Murder

Although James Ross had a house on the Forth and Clyde at lock 16, close to the village of Camelon, he was considered a stranger in the village. Locals were reluctant to admit him to their inner circle. The chief reason for his outsider status was his maritime occupation. Now twenty-six years of age, he had spent the majority of his youth and young adult life as a crewman on sailing vessels. It further counted against him that he wasn't a native, having been born in the fishing village of Burghead on the Moray Firth. His physical characteristics may have been considered off-putting by some. He had a dark complexion and bushy whiskers and although no taller than the average for the era, his build was strikingly solid and burly. A disapproving newspaper reporter would later describe him as an uncultivated man of forbidding appearance.

His connection with Camelon began in the year 1868 when he disembarked at Grangemouth harbour on a modest-sized boat named the Coquette. According to his drouthy custom Ross headed straight for the local hostelry, the Canal Inn, and struck up a high-speed relationship with a woman who was serving. A marriage took place within days. The new Mrs Ross had cause to regret the union. Her life had changed very little. She went on living with her mother while her spouse continued to spend most of his time at sea. On the rare occasions when her husband was on terra firma, locals nicknamed him "the Captain".

The couple had a house at George's Square on the north side of the canal, a little to the south of Camelon. It was known locally as Nailer's Square. Nail-making had been prevalent in the area as a result of demand from the nearby Carron Works, though the occupation's heyday was past. Life in the square was nobody's idea of luxurious. The buildings grouped around it were a mix of workshops, old forges and humble dwellings that were small and dark. The Ross's house comprised one apartment and a small garret with a single window and door looking on to the outside world. The local newspaper, the *Falkirk Herald*, labelled the housing "wretched".

On the Christmas Eve of 1870, a Saturday, the square looked a little brighter and there was some cause for good spirits among the inhabitants. Snow had fallen and it lay crisply about. A number of locals had taken advantage of the freezing weather to stage an outdoor curling match. Ross had got employment as a labourer at a chemical works to the west of lock 16 and the couple now had a six-month old baby. The chemical workers, including the Captain, were paid at two o'clock in the afternoon and after they finished at six o'clock their time would be their own. His work done, Ross went to Falkirk. He then returned to Camelon but, in keeping with his aversion to a settled life, avoided his wife and baby. He went directly to another house in Nailer's Square to join a small party of men who were drinking. The host was shoemaker George Henry who, not to be outdone for a nickname, was known as "Poodles".

By all accounts the do at Poodles' place remained good-natured and the liquor flowed freely. If the Captain was beginning to feel accepted by the villagers, this was about to be halted abruptly by a visit from Mrs Ross. Her frustration with her husband's wanderings was rising. A neighbour had told her of his whereabouts and she couldn't bear the thought that he was drinking away his earnings while she stayed at home with the baby. She set off for Poodles' house to persuade her husband to come home. On arrival she met him at the top of the stair. Poodles and the company saw words fly between the couple with mounting ire, until Mrs Ross dished out a slap to the side of her husband's face. This humiliation appeared to flick a switch in him. He moved to retaliate, but failed to land the hit. His wife fled, uttering terrified cries of "Murder!" with the Captain hot on her heels. Moulder James Craig was in the square at the time with three other young men. Craig noticed with a chill that he was brandishing a knife and cursing that he would get revenge—his wife or someone else would be on the receiving end of it, he said. Craig said to him, "Mate, you should command your passion or you'll get into trouble."

The Captain arrived at his house to find the door locked. This made him angrier still, and he tried to get in by the window, breaking the shutter and smashing the glass. The noise drew the attention of a man who lived close to the square, Henry McGeney. A nail-maker of Irish extraction, McGeney was married with five children. He had been a participant in the curling match. Earlier that fateful evening McGeney had done a turn as a Good Samaritan, helping an old man who slipped in the snow to get up and make his way safely home. Although well-regarded by villagers, he had notched up convictions for poaching and rumour had it that he had served time for breach of the peace.

When the window-breaking occurred, McGeney had been on his way home and was exchanging a few words with Craig and his friends.

They group moved nearer to the Captain's house, but McGeney was the one who made the mistake of getting involved. Ross had successfully broken into his own house but his wife was absent and he now wanted to get out of it. McGeney gave him the common-sense advice to come out as he had gone in—through the window. When he refused to do so, McGeney said he would help him out the door. The pair combined forces to get the door open. As soon as he was out in the snow, the Captain turned his rage on the others. The young men fled and there were words between the remaining pair. McGeney dropped a piece of broken shutter he had been holding and took to his heels. For the second time that night a chase was on. Unfortunately, the nail-maker got his foot caught in a drain and fell, enabling his pursuer to grab him and force him down. Within moments McGeney was heard shouting that Ross was shoving a knife into him. "Tam, come and help, I'm stabbed," he cried, beckoning a young man called Thomas Smith. But Smith was too afraid of Ross to approach.

The incident had happened close to the house of a family with the appropriate name of Risk. Eighteen-year-old Alexander had been out in the square and briefly considered pulling the two men apart while they grappled on the ground, but his step-mother had urged him back inside and bolted the door. Now they heard McGeney's weakened voice calling, "Let me in." Cautiously, the Risks opened the door. Henry McGeney was lying on a huge crimson-stained patch of snow, bleeding profusely. He fainted into the arms of the young man, who pulled him in from the cold and laid him down. The injured man pleaded for someone to get a napkin and stem the blood flowing from his throat. A few minutes later he gave up the ghost.

News of the tragedy spread quickly. A crowd gathered outside the Risk house and Sergeant Nixon arrived from Falkirk with two constables. The officers noted the pool of blood and the cadaver of McGeney. Trying Ross's door, they entered to find him in bed. Remarkably, he seemed to be in deep slumbers. The officers then noted a few pieces of evidence. There was torn clothing with blood stains on it and bloody fingerprints marked a wall by the door. Most incriminating was a knife with a three-inch blade, which was wet and beside it, a bucket full of sandy water. Ross was handcuffed and led away. Meanwhile, his wife was hiding out at her mother's house.

The post-mortem was carried out by Drs Hamilton and Moffat from Falkirk. Their report described five stab wounds on McGeney's body: on a hip, on a forearm, under an armpit, beneath a shoulder and, fatally, on the left side of the neck. That last wound had severed the carotid artery, causing the rapid blood flow that led to the nail-maker's death. The press speculated as to what could have lain at the heart of this peculiarly violent incident. Was it revenge? Had there been pre-existing rivalry between the Captain and McGeney?

In early May 1871, the circuit court arrived in Stirling with its customary pomp. The great men of the law, buoyed along with a procession of military attire and music, were greeted by the town officials. The court room was packed with people intrigued by the Christmas murder. The four young men who were in the square gave evidence. James Craig related the prelude to the violence in which the Captain chased his terrified wife across the square, and observed that he seemed more agitated than drunk. Two members of the group, 18-year-old Thomas Smith and 17-year-old William Gardiner, largely concurred with Craig's evidence. Gardiner had heard McGeney speak the ominous words: "I'll soon get you out. I don't care for your knife." Smith emphasised that the four of them had fled the scene because they were very much afraid. Peter Bain, 18, revealed that he had been pursued by Ross briefly, although he had done nothing to provoke him.

Alexander Risk stated that McGeney had been on his way to his own house, and wasn't chasing Ross. It was Ross who had broken the shutter and, although McGeney held the piece of wood for two or three minutes, he didn't brandish it. Both Alexander and Mrs Risk painted McGeney's character in a positive light, describing him as an amiable sort. Mrs McGeney identified the ripped clothing as belonging to her late husband. She described him as a peaceable man and stated that although he had been caught poaching, he had never done time in prison for breach of the peace. Sergeant Nixon described the scene that had greeted him and the constables on arrival in Ross's house in the early hours of the Sunday morning: the suspect in bed, the torn clothes and the wet knife. The blade had sand and clay stuck to it—just like the dirty mixture in the bucket. Nixon believed Ross had washed the blood off in an attempt to conceal his involvement.

The accused declared that although he had taken some whisky he hadn't been drunk that night. He offered a different version of events from the witnesses. He had entered the house by the window, breaking off part of the shutter because the door was locked and he wanted to get to bed. Once inside, he removed his boots by the fire. He had taken hold of a knife in order to cut tobacco, then heard the clamour of a crowd outside, all asking to get in. When he told them the door was locked they had smashed their way in and one aimed a blow at him with a stick. He had pursued a man into the square, admittedly still clutching the knife. The pair fell and grappled in the snow, but he remembered little of that. He returned home without seeing anything more of the other man. He made the surprising claim that he didn't know McGeney at all. Although he'd had a house in Nailer's Square for two years, he hadn't lived there for more than eight months. He really didn't know the place at all. He also had no idea why a crowd of people had gathered outside his house, wishing to force their way in. He painted a picture of a stranger in a close-knit community.

The Advocate Depute Mr Balfour, addressing the jury for the prosecution, said the evidence clearly showed that the prisoner had inflicted the wounds on McGeney, thereby causing his death. There could be no doubting it was a case of wilful murder. Foul name-calling or slight assault would never constitute an excuse for taking another man's life. Mr Campbell, for the defence, argued that McGeney had brought the attack on himself. He claimed that the nail-maker was the aggressor: he had gone to the house of the prisoner with the intention to quarrel, had broken open the door and wielded the shutter-wood. He urged the jury to return a verdict for the lesser offence of culpable homicide. In summing up, the Lord Justice-Clerk asked the jury to consider the role provocation might have played.

Had it been the prisoner's intention to start a quarrel or to quell one? The jury returned after just five minutes with a unanimous verdict of culpable homicide. The Captain was sentenced to five years' penal servitude, considerably less than expected. The stolid Ross remained unmoved. If he believed he had got off lightly, as the majority of onlookers did, he wasn't going to show it.

CHAPTER TWO: SAFE AS HOUSES

Conflict in the Making

This chapter delves into incidents, some of them dramatic and violent, that took place on canalside land and property. As the landscapes evolved and changed, so did the incidents that took place along the banks. Maps from the eighteenth and early nineteenth century feature mansion-style houses scattered throughout the lowlands and highlands, nestling amid sprawling private estates. Since these grand houses were sure to contain money, silver plate and other goodies, thieves would target them in operations carried out in the style of the classic country house robbery. Two such raids took place by the Union Canal within a decade. As the nineteenth century went on, thieves were drawn to humbler homes and to manufacturing complexes where cash and valuables were likely to be stored overnight. Intruders could do advance homework on the property's layout and the movements of its occupants by observing discreetly from the bank, and a boat tucked into bushes at the bottom of a garden would help to effect a smooth getaway.

A brief look back to the late eighteenth and early nineteenth century when the canals were first proposed, then dug across country, reveals regular outbreaks of conflict over land and property. Farmers and landowners saw canal company proposals to seize portions of their land as a threat. Sometimes the warring parties managed to resolve their differences through discussions about compensation, but it wasn't unknown for a furious landowner to take the law into his own hands. Sometimes landowners did all they could to squeeze compensation money out of the canal company. People who protested against canal-making have long been depicted as eccentric members of the awkward squad. But to be fair, their criticisms were sometimes valid, just like the contemporary householder who points out the damaging effects of development on the doorstep. Make no mistake, canal development was a colossal upheaval with permanent consequences.

The trauma was most likely to hit privileged folk who were accustomed to living in the peaceful surroundings of large gardens, often with an orchard, home farm and perhaps woodlands. With canal development came gangs of rough, hard-drinking, 'foreign' labourers, noisy machinery, heaps of excavated earth and the severing of land in two. A pastoral environment in the lowlands would be transformed into an industrial zone with boats belching coal-smoke. Passenger boats could bring hordes of gawping tourists drifting past the windows. In addition to the privacy loss, this incursion of workmen and tourists would prove to have implications for crime.

While the Forth and Clyde was in the making, violence threatened between the canal company and the Carron Iron Works. Ill feeling spiralled after the canal makers failed to honour a promise to construct a short waterway to serve the Carron Works, and a game of psychological ping-pong ensued. In defiance, the manager of the Carron Works, Charles Gascoigne, withheld the company's subscription payments from the canal. In 1775 the canal makers diverted a water supply away from the Carron towards the canal. Striking back, the Carron Works blocked a stream with rubble in order to remove the water source from the canal and restore it to their iron complex. When Robert Mackell, the canal's resident engineer, complained, Gascoigne vowed to "blow out the brains" of anyone who dared to take their water supply. Since the Carron Works was a world-leading manufacturer of cannon and ammunition, this was no idle threat. The matter was eventually resolved without violence, but goodwill remained in short supply.

Further north, there was conflict too. In 1798, saboteurs struck when the Aberdeenshire Canal was excavated between Inverurie and Aberdeen. Stones and rubbish were thrown into the cutting and boats and labourers' tools were damaged. The management committee warned that the culprits could be transported overseas for seven years, and offered a reward of £5 for information leading to a conviction. The threat of criminal charges was unsuccessful, since workmen were still complaining about being obstructed in 1802. Two years after that, work on the Caledonian Canal began. The prospect of the large-scale waterway passing through his lands dismayed the 15th chief of Clan MacDonell of Glengarry, a man who lived in the style of the clan chiefs of earlier times. Glengarry lived on Loch Oich and owned land for ten miles along the Great Glen. The Caledonian Canal would profoundly alter the landscape around his mansion house and affect his privacy, with tourist boats and trading ships plying to and fro along the previously quiet loch. The chief regarded the canal company's offers of money as paltry recompense and in September 1816, still dissatisfied with the response to his complaints, he decided to assert his interests physically.

Like the old chiefs of the former military society, Glengarry was wont to travel with a retinue. With thirty fully-armed Highlandmen he arrived at the east end of Loch Oich to protest. The party strode up to the canal labourers, threatened and intimidated them away from the works, stole a company boat and took it to Loch Garry, where they dumped it. The commissioners pressed for Glengarry to be charged with theft. Fortunately for the laird the commissioners, having recovered their boat, let the matter drop. As the final stages of the canal work went on within his lands, Glengarry demanded bridges and privacy screens. Like the Aberdeenshire objectors, he placed physical obstructions in the workmen's way, yet still managed to evade prosecution. On the waterway's official opening day in October 1822, he made a statement by gatecrashing as boats went down Neptune's Staircase to Fort William.

After Scotland's major canals were completed, the heated bickering subsided and crimes of a more serious character began. An incident on the banks of the Monkland Canal was inspired by animosity of the most personal sort—and the motive, revenge.

A Warning Shot

In late eighteenth-century Glasgow, stonemason Alexander Waddell was a pillar of the community. He got into bed at ten each night and rose at six every morning, ready to roll up his sleeves for any work that would come his way. He was three times elected deacon of the Masons' Guild, which made him the mouthpiece of his trade on the council. Within a few years, the building firm he'd set up with partner Matthew Park was securing valuable contracts from the city magistrates to construct a market for the trading of fresh produce, St George's Tron Church, and the court buildings and jail at the Saltmarket. From these endeavours, Mr Waddell made "a guid lump o' money." A man with a commanding physical presence, he dressed in striking clothes and sported a larger-than-average hat. He used his "lump o' money" to build himself an imposing mansion in the Gorbals looking across the River Clyde towards Glasgow Green, close to where a street named after him still exists. He named it Stonefield and installed his wife Elizabeth and two servants. Beggars would often call at the door, as word had got abroad that he was something of a philanthropist. His nearby farm grew potatoes and meal.

But Mr Waddell's affairs merited a second look. Rumour had it that his success resulted from making the most of a particular friendship with Glasgow's Lord Provost. It was said that in Elizabeth he'd found a true soulmate, for she shared his fondness for driving a hard bargain. To save on the heating bills at Stonefield, the self-made man, wife and servants crammed themselves into one apartment, leaving the rest of the house unheated and overtaken by cobwebs. As for the destitute people who went to the door, they would certainly be helped to potatoes and meal—providing they put their hands in their pockets and paid handsomely for it. Some of those who had direct financial dealings with him declared him to be a miser of the worst kind.

In the year 1812, money continued rolling into the coffers from the civic contracts and farming concerns. Waddell's enterprising eye began to rove further afield. It drifted a few miles east of the city and alighted on the Monkland Canal, which was then doing brisk business sending coal into Glasgow and Edinburgh along the Forth and Clyde and Union Canals. Waddell snapped up lands near the canal bank where a seam of good quality workable coal lay, which would be ripe for extraction and sale. Above ground the centrepiece was

Heatheryknowe, a good-sized house set amid lawns and vegetable gardens and surrounded by a discreet screen of trees, making it a worthy country seat. Its master bedroom was on the south the side of the house, with a window looking over the gardens. Also within the gardens, though at arm's length, was a smaller house named Auchenlonen. An unpleasant smell hung around Waddell's dealings with Heatheryknowe and Auchenlonen. In the process of making the purchase he had put a number of local noses out of joint, not least among the Scott family, who had formerly owned and farmed Heatheryknowe. The Scotts then moved into Easter House, which lay to the south and would later give its name to the housing estate we know today. The family consulted a lawyer regarding their concerns that there was something underhand about the sale. The Scotts and their neighbours the Muirs lived within a tight circle of folk who inhabited the local farms; many were related to each other by blood or marriage and eking a living out of the land was a communal undertaking. John Scott and his brother-in-law Archibald Muir now found themselves dependent on the new laird of Heatheryknowe for their living. After Waddell began mining operations in the area, they bought coal from him and set up as coal merchants trading on the canal, with assistance from John Scott junior and his nephew Gavin. For their business to succeed they relied heavily on the coalowner to deal them a fair hand and in time they came to the view that he could not necessarily be relied on to do so. Throughout 1818 it became increasingly apparent that Scott and Muir were struggling to pay their debts. By the autumn they were bankrupt.

The situation took a dramatic turn on Friday, 20th November 1818 when Alexander Waddell came from Stonefield to visit his country seat. He spent the day pottering about Heatheryknowe Farm, then went indoors to see if his favourite dish of potato and salt herring was on the menu. The evening ticked by and he got into bed at his customary hour of ten o'clock. Sometime between midnight and 1 o'clock in the morning Waddell's sleep was disturbed by a loud report as though from a gun. After some time he decided it was safe to get out of bed to investigate. He went to the window and held a candle to the shutter. There, lodged in the wood, was a ball of lead like one that would be shot from a gun. The ball had shattered the window pane but failed to get any further because of the shutter. Waddell reflected that he had neglected to close the shutter, the bullet would have hit him—he would have been injured or perhaps killed. Whoever fired had known precisely where in the room he would be sleeping, and therefore had intended to give him more than a mere warning. Day dawned and Waddell rose at 6 o'clock. He went into the gardens and looked carefully under the window. There were footprints in one of the flower beds—the prints of a full-grown man. The track could be traced to the southern boundary wall, but disappeared beyond that.

The stonemason reported the incident to the police and gave a statement summarising the events of the night. In an irate tone he protested his bafflement as to why on earth any person would wish to see him dead. This protest was rather disingenuous given the controversial nature of his business affairs. In any case, the police quickly moved to arrest John Scott, Gavin Scott and Archibald Muir. The trio were taken to the tollbooth of Glasgow where they were detained for a time, then released. Waddell returned to draughty Stonefield and attempted to put the whole business out of his mind. But if he thought that was going to be the end to it, he would be disappointed. On the morning of 25th December 1818 (a date not then celebrated as it is now) the stonemason opened his post to find a note. Its message was distinctly unpleasant. The writer accused Waddell of being "an incorrigible, avaricious tyrant" who had wronged sundry persons in the Monklands and Glasgow area.

" …I have paid attention to your horrid conduct these past ten years (said the note), and your cup is now full and you shall drink it… I can think of no dead (deed) more glorious that I can perform than to relieve the oppressed by putting a tyrant to death."

Statements were taken from all who worked at Scott and Muir Coal Merchants, and it was briefly entertained that Muir might have penned the letter while in prison. But no one had seen him writing during this time, and suspicion fell on Gavin Scott. A sample of his handwriting was taken and compared with the letter. There was sufficient similarity that it was decided he must have penned the letter after he got out of prison. Furthermore, this suggested that he was likely to have been the person who fired the shot through the window, even if it could not be proved. Members of the Scott family gave statements in support of the accused man. They said that on the night of the botched shooting Gavin Scott had been at Easter House farmhouse on the Friday afternoon and spent the night fast asleep on the put-me-down bed in the kitchen. A gun was kept hanging to the left of the kitchen door, but it had remained there, unused, throughout the night.

Waddell must have been well aware that some had taken exception to his high-handed financial dealings. The signs are that he was putting together a master plan to amass a large stretch of land along the banks of the Monkland Canal by means that were not entirely admirable. However, he continued to maintain that the outrage was out of all proportion to any perceived offence on his part. He was convinced that Gavin Scott had been guilty, perhaps acting with others of his clan. Scott does not appear to have been sentenced to more than a second term of imprisonment at the Tolbooth. Perhaps the charge was dropped owing to lack of evidence. For the Scott family, the loss of their family home would be punishment enough.

The Spanish Cloak

In December 1825, the waters of the Union Canal hadn't frozen solid, though the weather was remarkably cold. Coal boats travelled briskly, as usual, between Port Hopetoun and the Duke of Hamilton's Colliery at Redding. Close to the banks on a quiet stretch between Falkirk and Linlithgow was Muiravonside Manse, home to 60-year-old Reverend William McCall and two young servants, Janet Roberts and Elizabeth Taylor. At about 1 o'clock in the morning of Sunday 11th, McCall stirred. From his bedroom he had heard the sounds of someone moving around downstairs. It wasn't unknown for visiting ministers to arrive from Edinburgh by night boat, but he wasn't expecting anyone. Most likely, a servant was going on with some domestic task into the small hours.

McCall was still awake when a louder noise startled him. He hauled himself out of bed and opened the door a crack to see that more than one shadowy figure was moving about in flickering candlelight. Suddenly, the situation became all too clear. Two men rushed up the stairs towards him, one brandishing a pistol and the other a sword, and a voice growled: "If ye don't give up your money I'll shoot ye." A third person of slighter build, who was dressed like a sailor or boatman, stayed halfway down the stairs. In the dim light of the candle he carried the pistol-bearer appeared to be dressed, quite surreally, in a Spanish cloak.

The intruders shouted and intimidated the clergyman into leading them to a chest of drawers. They turned the key in the lock and set about ransacking it. Inside was a handkerchief containing money collected from parishioners for the deaf and dumb institution, amounting to £5. After claiming the charity money they stripped a larger chest of the shirts and stockings it contained and bundled them up together. Unfortunately for the Reverend McCall, the thieves spotted one of his prized possessions, a gold watch from George Gowell of London, which he had left at the window. The only thing they didn't find was his own money, which he had earlier wrapped up in a pantaloon. The man with the sword raised the point to McCall's cheek and threatened to use it on him. The minister, who was not in the best of health, grew very afraid, as there was a ruthlessness to this man's manner that suggested he wouldn't hesitate to kill anyone who got in his way. However, the accomplice put up a restraining hand and said: "It's only money we want—we'll not hurt ye." With this gesture, the man in the Spanish cloak may have saved the clergyman's life.

The intruders forced him to lead them downstairs to join the man who had waited behind. In the parlour there was talk of trussing McCall, although they didn't carry out this threat. They opened a press and found a silver tea pot and other antiques, most of which they ignored, with the exception of silver teaspoons marked "W M". Their next port of call on the ground floor was the dining room, where all three turned their attention to a cupboard—and their backs to McCall. Seizing his moment, the clergyman made a dash through the hall, fumbled at the lock on the front door and ran as fast as he could across the churchyard and the fields to the farmhouse at Haining nearby. The farmer, a Mr Reid, armed himself and summoned his two servants, and the group made its way to the manse. They got there to find that the intruders had fled into the night—surely by boat—and the servants had come downstairs from their sleeping quarters in the garret. Janet Roberts had seen the intruders leading her master downstairs and observed that the one who waited on the stairs was slighter than the other two. She had heard a voice use the phrase "make haste" shortly before the opening of the front door.

Now that the thieves were gone it emerged that this had not been an entirely slick operation. The haul comprised all the deaf and dumb collection money save a few halfpennies, nine teaspoons, some shirts and the grey stockings, which Reverend McCall had received in a present; but in their hurry to get away the housebreakers had left a number of items behind. Close to the window a small chisel and horseshoe were found, used respectively to remove putty from the frame and to smash the glass. A few shirts and teaspoons had been dropped. Indiscreetly, the thieves had left personal items that might help lead to their identification: two spotted cotton handkerchiefs and an old hat bearing the label Mackay Cunningham, Edinburgh. The trio would be escaping along the Union Canal, so time was of the essence. The Sheriff substitute for Linlithgow, James Rae, took a statement from the Reverend McCall as quickly as he could in order to catch the next mail to Stirling and alert the procurator fiscal there as to what had happened. Still unsettled from his ordeal, the clergyman gave sketchy descriptions of the men, details of the objects taken and what they had left behind. Rae remarked in a footnote to the fiscal that the offenders were thought to have gone west with a load of coal; and two of them had worn the sort of strong "tacketted" shoes characteristic of the labouring classes.

Straight away the search was on and from early on Sunday morning inquiries were made among boat crews that had been operating in the vicinity of Falkirk and Linlithgow. Later on, sheriff-officers arrived at Kingscavil Quarry, east of Linlithgow, and began searching all the boats. One vessel, No. 61, was at the time heading eastwards to the Duke of Hamilton's coal depot at Edinburgh, and was ordered to go no further. The master, twenty-seven-year-old Edward Quin, complied. He berthed alongside the quarry so that the officers could begin searching. Almost immediately one of the officers had found something in the coals: a pair of stockings bearing the initials W M. The officers marked the stockings with ink because they would be used as evidence. Sitting next to them was a bushy-haired young man named John McGraddy. He and Quinn were apprehended.

An inventory was compiled of the ten items that were retained in custody in relation to the Muiravonside manse robbery: a sword, a pistol, an old greatcoat with metal buttons, an old hat, a pair of light grey worsted stockings, a blue and white spotted handkerchief, a red-and-yellow handkerchief, a horseshoe and a small chisel. There was also a book called *The Readiest Reckoner*. A fresh, more detailed statement was taken from the Reverend McCall, who'd had time to reflect on his impressions of the turn of events. He estimated that the men had been in the house for fifteen minutes, and the way they pronounced the word "money" strongly suggested that they were Irish. The further observations he made would prove to have a decisive effect on the ultimate outcome of the case. He was confident that if he saw the man who held the pistol again, he would recognise him. As for the garment this man wore, he had revised his initial impression that it was a Spanish cloak. He now believed it had been a coat in exceptionally poor condition—extremely tattered about the edges. This observation fitted with testimony given by another witness, Robert Snowden. Snowden operated machinery on the banks of the canal that was used for raising and lowering large quantities of coal, a station that meant he saw almost all the vessels going by. He had often seen McGraddy and Quin on boat No. 61 and, shown the coat that had been taken into custody, said he recognised it as one worn by Edward Quin.

In his statement, Quin had said that he and McGraddy had set out from Edinburgh on boat No. 61 on the Friday night preceding the robbery. They had not been in any house between Saturday night and Sunday morning and hadn't left the boat, except for a brief period when they got on board the coal boat No. 63 and warmed themselves by its fire. On the Sunday morning they had left Redding to return to Edinburgh. He couldn't be sure that McGraddy had worn the stockings during the journey because he had long trousers but he was sure that, prior to the sheriff-officers finding them there, the stockings had not been among the coals in the boat. He saw McGraddy later in the day and he had clearly been drinking. They spoke about the burglary at the manse and the way McGraddy smirked inclined Quinn to think that he had somehow been involved.

Many of the men on the coal boats worked for the same employer and had intermarried to a large extent, and only two names had initially emerged. Now the enquiry widened in scope and other names came into the frame. On 23rd December the procurator fiscal at Stirling, John Sawers, issued a warrant for the apprehension and detention of two brothers called McEwan, Hugh and John, who had anglicised their name from McKeown. The McEwan brothers, who sailed boat No. 63, had been identified by a man called Alexander Brownfield or Alexander Pringle. Like Quin and McGraddy they were employees of the canal's largest coal merchant, James Dawson. The brothers were duly arrested and detained at the Stirling tollbooth, despite the fact that Brownfield was described as "a bad character" and was therefore regarded as an unreliable witness.

John McGraddy admitted to involvement in the robbery and named Charles Clark and Peter 'Pate' O'Donnel, one of whom had been on the stairs, and the other outside the back door. The chisel belonged to Clark, he said, but the prime mover in the crime was John Curran. Curran was a fellow boatman (who went by the alias Corran). For months he had been getting work on any boat he could find as the vessel he usually used was being repaired. The whole thing had been Curran's idea and he had most active during the robbery. Curran had broken the kitchen window and was the one who wielded the sword, terrifying Reverend McCall, and McGraddy had intervened by holding his hand up. In other words, McGraddy was admitting to being the man in the tattered garment that looked like a Spanish cloak. He asked the fiscal to allow him to turn King's evidence, an arrangement that would mean he could fully disclose all the facts in return for immunity from prosecution.

The case was becoming more complicated by the minute. Scores of pages of evidence were accumulated by the legal men, and extensive deliberations were taking place as to what approach should be taken in the court. Sawers believed that this was a very important case so they must get it right. He believed that there was a gang of Irishmen at work, men who were afforded the privilege of easy access to the house by means of the canal. Some of the boatmen stopped at the manse to get milk about once a week. Indeed, McGraddy had done so on the Wednesday before the robbery, according to the servant Elizabeth Taylor. Of the four men now in custody—McGraddy, Quin and the McEwan brothers—Sawers believed that only the first had been involved in the commission of the crime. The other three who had carried it out, Charles Clarke, Pate O'Donnell and John Curran, had gone on the run. According to McGraddy, Curran had taken all the stolen items, to Edinburgh he thought, and had gone to ground ever since. For several weeks, attempts to find and apprehend the missing trio proved unsuccessful.

The case began to liven up once the trail crossed the sea to Ireland. A man called Gallagher had tried to sell a watch answering the description of Reverend McCall's at a town named Ballibofey in County Donegal. Gallagher, whether that was his real name or not, was pursued by the authorities for some 60 miles across wild country, but got away. However, Curran was found hiding out at a house in Lifford. He was handcuffed and led across a field. He said to the sheriff-officer not to treat him so roughly and enquired whether he had heard "anything against him from Scotland".

At the High Court held in Stirling on 20th April, McGraddy and Curran were charged with stouthrief (housebreaking aggravated by use or threat of violence against a householder) and theft. McGraddy was not permitted to turn King's evidence. Instead, Edward Quin, even though he was considered to have had some involvement in the gang's operation, proved to be a key witness. There was bad blood between McGraddy and Quin, though Quin claimed, somewhat disingenuously, that this would not affect his testimony against the other man. The Reverend McCall appeared, to confirm the items that had been taken from the manse. Janet Roberts concurred that the men had sounded Irish; and *The Readiest Reckoner* contained conversion tables from Scottish to Irish currency, which would clearly be useful for anyone re-selling stolen goods. It emerged that McGraddy hadn't had the easiest start in life. He'd been orphaned at a tender age and was said to be a little backward as a result of a heavy blow to the head in childhood. He was a strapping man whose build made him better suited to the work than some and, it was said, was handsome. During lean times in Scotland he, like Curran, would return to Ireland in search of work. He had no previous convictions.

Margaret McEwan, wife of Edward Quinn and a relative of the two of the same name, declared that she had heard John Curran boast "I'll drink a bottle of wine before this day fortnight and have £50 in my pocket." She had considered it a jest at the time, but now took it as an indication of his planning the robbery. Perhaps the repairs to Curran's boat had reduced his earnings or left him idle and stirred in him a certain desperation. While in Ireland several warrants had been issued against Curran for riotous behaviour. When the old hat left behind at the manse had been tried on the heads of all the suspects, it was thought that it fitted Curran better than anyone else.

Despite the evidence that he had been the planner, was trying to sell the stolen goods and had been in trouble with the law in Ireland after the robbery, jury found Curran Not Guilty. McGraddy, however, was pronounced Guilty; and the sentence he was allotted by Lord Mackenzie turned his legs to jelly. He was sentenced him to be hanged by the neck until dead. Gasps went up all round the court, as it was virtually unheard of for a first-time offender to be sentenced to execution. The devastated man had to be carried from the bar. It may be speculated that this harsh treatment reflected that the victim had been a clergyman and one of the perpetrators a lowly Irishman. The authorities were determined to make an example of this gang of Irish thieves operating on the canal and selling goods elsewhere. For all they knew, there could be other gangs taking advantage of the proximity of certain houses to the canal. They were determined to knock this sort of crime on the head, no matter how unjust this might be to the individual punished. Efforts to obtain clemency for McGraddy swung into operation. The Provost and Magistrates of Stirling collectively submitted a petition. His employer, James Dawson and a Mr McGibbon, the keeper of Stirling jail, wrote testifying to his good character; and the clergyman reiterated his belief that the man in the "Spanish cloak" had saved him from death at the hands of his more ruthless accomplice.

The pleas fell on deaf ears. At two o'clock on Friday, 26th May, the condemned man finished his prayers, reluctantly left the jail and ascended the scaffold before the crowd that had gathered on Broad Street, Stirling. McGraddy dropped the white handkerchief from his hand, the signal that he would now submit to the hand fate had dealt him.

An Unwanted Mansion

In time, particular places came to be associated with canal crimes in the public mind. The mansion house of Glenfuir, Falkirk, came to notice in the autumn of 1835 when it was targeted by a notorious Edinburgh gang. Before this the house had a very chequered history, and the canal company had probably begun to wonder whether the place was jinxed. Lieutenant-Colonel William Duncan had snapped it up at the turn of the nineteenth century, and had every reason to be contented. He had a working farm, generous fruit and vegetable growing areas, a state-of-the-art network of pipes for carrying water indoors and twenty-one apartments and servants' accommodation. Then the Union Canal Committee came along in 1813 with its proposal to cut the waterway nearby. The committee wanted to buy a small tranche of the estate in order to link the new canal with lock sixteen of the Forth and Clyde. But Duncan was furious. The company could fork out to buy the entire estate at a premium, or go away empty-handed. Following a long and tough campaign, the military man prevailed in the end. He got an impressive 12,000 Guineas from the canal builders for a house and 60 acres of land that were largely no use. With this princely payment, the Colonel bought a property in Dublin. There he developed an addiction to laudanum and ended up dying in squalor in an Irish debtors' prison.

During the making of the canal, Colonel Duncan's state-of-the-art water system proved to be a nuisance. The diggers and the masons who had the task of creating the eleven locks complained that a seemingly endless network of pipes hampered their progress. By 1822, the great house now found itself close to two canal features: the 'dark tunnel' that ran under Prospect Hill, and the eleven locks linking with the Forth and Clyde. While boats went through the tedious process of navigating the locks, passengers would disembark at Glenfuir, walk or take a cart a short distance, then swap to another vessel. The Union Canal Company decided to advertise the house as an inn where passengers changing could enjoy refreshments. The plan failed because no agreement could be reached with the Forth and Clyde Canal Company. The company then tried to make money from the house by flogging some of the contents, including four-poster beds, mirrors, china and crystal. After many years of advertising the house, a tenant eventually came along, but the premises struggled to pay its way as an inn.

By 1835, however, it appeared that Glenfuir House was entering a happier period. It had been purchased by John Morehead, the collector of customs at the busy port of Grangemouth. Morehead belonged to a Stirlingshire dynasty that had risen to note in East India and had achieved distinction in the medical profession. He was a member of the Speculative Society, to which a number of Edinburgh's literary luminaries had been admitted, not least Sir Walter Scott. The house was no longer an inn. Morehead filled it with a fine silverware collection and sometimes brought considerable quantities of cash home with him. On Wednesday, 7th October, he brought home the sum of £41, some in £1 notes and the remainder in fives from the Bank of Scotland. These he placed in the drawer of a table in his dining room, burying them among letters and papers for safety's sake. At about 11 o'clock he satisfied himself that the windows and doors in the lower apartments were secure, and went upstairs to bed.

Early the following morning, the servant, Robert Thomson, came down from his accommodation in the garret and realised that all was not well: the stairwell window was open. Thomson ran downstairs to investigate and there his worst fears were confirmed. Someone had entered the house and thrown the ground floor into confusion, removing some items and turning others upside-down. Thomson called his master. Morehead made straight for the dining room, and there his fears were confirmed. The thieves had removed the drawer from the table, strewn the letters and papers all over the floor and helped themselves to the money. With increasing trepidation, the collector turned to the sideboard, where he kept his valuable collection of silver-plated goods. The thieves had cleaned out silver salvers, spoons, fish slices, forks and wine funnels were all gone. Morehead sent for the police.

Officer Mowat arrived at the scene and began gathering information. With Morehead's help he made a list of everything that had been removed from the house, then went into the gardens to look for clues. Around the back, a box had been left below a kitchen window, showing where the thieves had made their entry. Walking round the house, he discovered two pairs of footsteps that didn't belong to any of the occupants, one large and one smaller. Mowat followed them across the sprawling lawns towards the muddy canal bank and on the way, came across the missing sideboard drawer. But he could see no sign of the loot. The policeman knew that houses and shops had been broken into and plundered by an audacious gang of thieves operating in the Edinburgh area for the last fifteen months. He thought it likely that this break-in was the work of the same gang, with the canal affording them an all-too convenient means of escape.

Officer Mowat was not the only one to have a busy morning. About four miles to the east along the Union Canal, long before the sun would come up, boatmaster James Ross had been in his coal vessel at Redding Colliery. Out of the darkness, two strangers approached with a curious request. They asked if he would be good enough to accompany them for a drink somewhere nearby. In the convivial surroundings of Learmonth's public house they offered to give Ross a pound, if he would do them a small favour. What they wanted was an alibi: should anyone came asking questions, Ross was to say that they had been aboard his boat all night. The master glanced down at their shoes. They were wet and muddy, as though they had been travelling on the canal. All the same, he nodded and took the money. Time would tell whether he would keep his word. Some hours later, the same two men were boarding a cart at Redding bound for Linlithgow. By this time news of the Glenfuir robbery was getting around, but when asked by the carter whether they had heard about it, but they fell strangely silent, as though they hadn't heard him speak at all. They did volunteer, however, that they were going on Edinburgh to visit some old friends. At 10 o'clock they a boarded a further cart for the metropolis.

The next day in Edinburgh, one of this pair entered the jeweller's shop of Thomas Picken in the West Bow and looked at his collection of timepieces. This time he was in the company of a taller fellow. They each bought two fine watches that came to £3 10s which they paid for with a Bank of Scotland pound note. On the Friday, Ross noticed the same pair of strangers back at Learmonth's public house, in company with the third, taller man who seemed to be a close associate. The trio resurfaced together early on the morning of Saturday, 10th October, when they boarded the Dasher passage boat on the Union Canal. Captain John Brock would eye them with increasing suspicion throughout the journey. One of trio, James McLaren, carried an unwieldy-looking bundle apparently stuffed with straw, which he was regarding carefully. His companion, Conley Gurney, wore a wristwatch that looked to be some way above his means, and paid for the passage with a Bank of Scotland pound note for which Brock and his crew could not find enough change. The tallest of the three, William Wilkie, also wore an impressive watch. The trio had boarded the Dasher at Lock No. 1, just a hundred yards from Glenfuir, which was the talk of the place following the robbery.

Gurney drank steadily all the way, talked non-stop and showed largesse to all the other passengers by offering drinks all round. By the time the boat arrived in Port Dundas some hours later, Gurney had lain his head down and fallen into a deep sleep. McLaren asked the boatmen if Gurney could be allowed to remain asleep on the boat. When John Brock agreed, McLaren did an odd thing. He removed the sleeping man's watch, then put his hands into his pockets and pulled out a large wad of notes. He kept the watch, but asked the steward's assistant, Archibald Malcolm, too look after the money and the straw-stuffed package for him. At this point Brock demanded that McLaren tell him what was in the package. McLaren mumbled that it was nothing but a couple of shirts before going away for a drink with Wilkie. McLaren said they would call back to collect his things at 5 o'clock.

The captain went off too. In his absence, Archibald Malcolm and the boat's mate, William Napier, began regarding the package with increasing suspicion. Napier agreed that there was something odd about it; the bundle was a great deal heavier than he would have expected for a pack of shirts—and hadn't there been some sort of crime committed at Glenfuir house only days before? Archibald was coming to the macabre presumption that a dead body was likely hidden inside it, just when a police officer named Russell arrived. Russell had been sent on the suspicions of John Brock. He examined the bundle and found items of silverware. He then asked the junior boatmen to tie it up exactly as it had been, so that the owner would suspect nothing when he came back. Sure enough, Wilkie and McLaren came back to collect the package. They asked for drink but were refused. Gurney was now awake so they were all taken into custody at the police office. The trial, which took place the following January at the High Court, was widely reported in the newspapers. James McLaren and Conley Gurney were charged with breaking into the mansion house of Glenfuir and stealing £41 in Bank of Scotland notes and a quantity of silverplate on the night of the 6th or the morning of 7th October 1835. The charge was aggravated by the fact that McLaren had been a thief by habit and repute for twelve months, and Gurney for eight. Both pleaded not guilty. Among the witnesses were the boatman Ross, who went back on his word, and Thomas Picken, the Edinburgh jeweller.

William Wilkie also appeared as a witness, issuing a series of denials. He had not entered the boat at Glenfuir House with the other two; though he had once been in Mr Picken's shop, that was not with Conley Gurney buying wristwatches; and he had taken no part in the robbery. On the night of the 7th October, said he, he'd slept in his mother's house at Castle Wynd in Edinburgh the whole night. Wilkie was asked whether he wished to proceed with his account, which contained several contradictions, and he persisted, so was put on record. However, the Lord Justice Clerk warned him that he was in danger of being transported for life if he committed perjury. At this warning, Wilkie hesitated and finally admitted that he had been in the prisoners' company after all following the theft, and that his previous testimony had been a lie.

Though no evidence was offered in court, Wilkie was thought to have been involved. It emerged during the trial that the stolen silverware had been buried in the ground at a spot close to Glenfuir, though Officer Mowat had been unable to find it at the time. Wilkie had returned with MacLaren and Gurney three days later to collect it, and of course he was known to have accompanied them to Glasgow on the Dasher. In all likelihood, Wilkie was a fellow member of the Edinburgh gang, the rest of whom remained at large. The spate of burglaries would go on apace throughout the winter, causing concern among householders and business people. The judge declared Wilkie guilty of prevarication upon oath and sentenced him to three months in the Bridewell, where he would be put to hard labour. MacLaren and Gurney did not get off so lightly. Police officers had checked their shoes against the prints that Officer Mowat had followed across the lawns of Glenfuir. The Lord Justice Clerk called the pair "heedlesss" and sentenced them to transportation for life.

Fool's Gold

By the early nineteenth century the industrial boom for the Lowland canals had been on the wane for some decades and the gangs of Irish boatmen that had struck such fear into the authorities the previous century had shrunk away. That did not mean to say, though, that the threat of crime to property and people along the banks had disappeared. In 1920s Edinburgh, Jean Lindsay was known to many as a seller of fish and fruit. Business was thriving. She lived with her daughter on Dorset Place in a mews house backing onto the Union Canal. Despite the house's proximity to busy parts of the city, its setting was surprisingly rustic. Adjoining the mews were a yard and stable, where Mrs Lindsay's chickens mingled with a few goats. The working day generally started early for the merchant, who would set off with her daughter to stock up the stall. One morning at the end of March, the pair set off just before 5am for Newhaven Fishmarket.

With the householders safely out of the way, an intruder appeared from his hiding place by the canal. He made straight for a back window, removed the lower pane and climbed in. He ignored the valuable watch and diamond ring that would have attracted the attention of the average thief. He had a specific haul in mind—a bag of gold in sovereigns and half sovereigns, which Mrs Lindsay had been amassing since 1914. The coins were regarded as part of the nation's gold reserves and were not generally treated as currency in Britain. The merchant's collection was worth £380.

The thief had learned that Mrs Lindsay kept the sovereigns in a leather bag inside a larger canvas bag, which was usually secreted halfway up the chimney behind a stove. He'd also gleaned that it had recently been moved from its usual place while cleaning went on. He put his hand on top of a wardrobe, feeling about, and there it was. He climbed out the window and made good his escape along the canal. It might be expected that the loss of the gold would be noticed straight way. But the room was seldom used, and it was only when the Lindsays went to check on the gold that the theft was discovered, along with the cut-away pane looking onto the canal. Straight away it was reported to the city police. The papers ran intriguing headlines such as "THE MISSING GOLD HOARD". The redoubtable Mrs Lindsay was quoted as saying she didn't really care if she never saw the money again, though she would happily hand out another hundred if she could just give thief "two biffs".

The thief was now left with the difficulty of disposing of his unusual haul. Perhaps it would be less conspicuous if he divided it into smaller amounts. Soon after the theft he walked into a bank on Leith Walk and placed the leather bag on the counter containing 45 of the sovereigns and ten of the half sovereigns. The teller, taken aback, asked how he had come by such a large amount in gold coins, and was told it had come from a firm of confectioners. This seemed to satisfy well enough, and he left with £50 in notes. The thief then toured other banks around Leith and Piershill and had more of the sovereigns exchanged for notes. At one bank in Trinity his luck began to run out. He arrived just half an hour after the staff. As he pushed the bag of gold across the counter, the teller eyed him suspiciously and asked where it had come from. He now came up with a story about a firm in Bonnington. The teller sprinted outside to fetch a policeman from the street, but they weren't quick enough; the man with the gold had fled.

The following morning the teller was brought to the police station and identified the man. He was one Henry Lee Dickson, a 21-year old who was familiar to Mrs Lindsay. On the week before she had employed him as a lorryman, carrying goods around the city. Although engaged on 30 shillings per week plus meals, he had left after only two days, for which she gave him 8 shillings. Naturally, his sudden departure had made him the prime suspect. The police managed to recover £55; Mrs Lindsay offered a reward for information leading to the outstanding amount.

When the case came to court at the end of July, the defence pointed out to the jury that the case rested upon the age-old challenge of identification. Only one of the bank tellers was able to identify Dickson as the man who had attempted to cash in the stolen hoard, and he had been able to say no more than "I know he is the man." The jury decided that the witness had got it right, and he was sentenced to 10 years in prison.

The Big Blow-up

The young men involved in this three-day escapade by the Monkland Canal could easily be mocked as bungling burglars, but there was a serious side to their actions. Not only did the lack of criminal expertise send their plans awry, it could have resulted in deaths or serious injuries. Fortunately, the Coatbridge Burgh Police managed to prevent the gang from proceeding to the most perilous part of their project, thanks to a night-time surveillance operation on the canal banks. Further danger arose, though, when the men attempted to flee. The long arm of the law would be needed to pluck them from danger a second time.

In the last hours of 1925, the iron and steel complexes sprawling along this stretch of the canal had fallen quiet. A number of premises were owned by Stewarts and Lloyds, a company started by two Lanarkshire brothers that now sent goods all over the world, and would eventually be part of British Steel. As a major employer in the area, Stewarts and Lloyds played a significant part in the town's social life. On the evening in question, 260 of its office staff were attending a dance and concert at the town hall, while a group of cadets met in the nearby Welfare Hall. It was the latter venue that the gang had in their sights.

The Welfare Hall was flanked by the old Crown Works, a maker of railway buffers, rivets and horseshoes fallen into disuse, and the huge Clyde Tube Works. Like many of the local works, they connected to the canal for the purpose of convenient transport, and all three buildings were owned by Stewarts and Lloyds. The cadets' meeting broke up without event. Once the coast was clear the four men appeared and applied their jemmy to the hall's entrance. The ringleader was 21-year-old brickworker William Gallacher. Gallacher could stake a claim to be the hard man of the gang. He was an able boxer and the possessor of a revolver, which he had left at home. His accomplices, like him local men in their twenties, were miner Alex McNaught and the Murphy brothers, Peter and Francis, who were both labourers.

Once inside, the men prised a secure box and drawer and helped themselves to pliers, a vice and a bunch of keys. Of most interest to them was the safe used by the cadets to store their savings; the difficulty, though, was how to open it. Since this prize would have to come with them, they pulled together and raised the safe, all 1½ hundredweights of it, up to window height and hurled it out. Where it landed was too visible from the Main Street for the gang's liking. They lugged it towards a wall on the west side of the complex and summoned further strength to raise it over a 20 feet high wall. It had fallen into the grounds of the old Crown Works—a better place, but still not good enough. The canal bank, they thought, would offer the best hiding place. They dragged the safe in a final 100-yard-dash across the Crown Works to the bed of a dried-up burn. It could stay there with the pliers, vice and coil, camouflaged by a covering of earth and branches, while they prowled the town for a means to open it.

In Dundyvan Road the gang jemmied the door of a second hall, forced open a cupboard and took £3. They had come to the conclusion that if they couldn't prise open the safe, they would have to blow it open. With that in mind, they broke into the explosives store of Rosehall colliery at Brewsterford, seizing an electric shot-exploder, coil, electric shot-firing cable, 50 detonators and 10lb of gelignite—a much larger quantity than necessary to explode the safe. Since day was dawning, they would have to bring their criminal enterprise to a close, for now. Over the next couple of days the gang sat tight, waiting for the right moment to carry out the next phase of their plan. A couple of them returned to the side to check discreetly that the safe was still there.

Midnight on Sunday, 3rd January, was the agreed time for the big blow-out. The men met promptly on the site armed with electric exploder and batteries, detonators, and gelatine. Unbeknown to them, Chief Constable McDonald had got his detectives on to the case soon after the burgling spree. A search had quickly revealed where the safe was camouflaged and officers had been keeping the canal bank under observation all along, including when the men went to check on their prize. With the four men clearly about to set an explosion, Constables

Dow and Donald broke cover, which prompted the burglars to make a run for it. With no easy escape route, all four men threw themselves into the canal. Within moments Gallacher and McNaught were in difficulty, flailing for all they were worth, shouting appeals to their accomplices and the police. There was no point in calling for the Murphy brothers. Peter and Francis had made it to the other side and were long gone. The rescue would be left to Dow and Donald alone. Although they were expert swimmers, it was a struggle getting both men onto the bank, and one came round only after artificial respiration.

Three weeks after this ordeal, the case was heard at Glasgow Sheriff Court. The Murphy brothers' successful flight had done them no good. Peter had given himself up and Francis was arrested in his home that night as he took off his soaked clothing. The court heard that the safe had contained £9, 9s, 10d, though the amount was academic as far as the burglars were concerned. They were charged with the three break-ins, and Gallacher was charged with possessing a revolver for which he had no licence. Each was imprisoned for six weeks. Sheriff Robertson said he had taken a lenient view. The men were unlikely to view the canal as useful escape route again. Canal crime in the twentieth century had changed, but it hadn't gone away.

CHAPTER THREE: SINS OF THE PEOPLE

The Linlithgow Hamper Mystery

Early on a Tuesday morning at the end of September 1930, farm servant James McNaughton was crossing a bridge over the Union Canal by Linlithgow when he noticed something unusual in the water. With farmer James Aitken, he was making his way to a field to inspect cut grain that had been gathered into bundles. The object McNaughton had spotted was some kind of package tied together with pieces of string, which floated close to the south bank. Once they were over the bridge he brought it to the side, placed it on the bank and cut the string. Two pieces of brown paper, both remarkably dry, had been drawn across the top of a straw hamper that might be used to carry groceries. Dreading that he was about to set eyes on a dead cat, he parted the paper to find a woman's pink dressing gown inside. Sticking out from its folds was a tiny human foot. He later told the *Linlithgow Gazette* what a terrible shock it had been.

The abandonment and murder of babies in Scotland's canals is a peculiarly disturbing subject. Although these occurrences were an open secret in the nineteenth and early twentieth centuries, the phenomenon is not acknowledged in the vast majority of canal histories. The discovery of an infant cadaver in the water was widespread and frequent, as is clear from the newspaper appeals for information that followed. Between 1800 and 1940 the bodies of at least 110 infants, most of them newborn, were reported as found in Scotland's canals, though reports fall dramatically during World War II, when newspapers were discouraged from printing gloomy stories that might damage morale. In reality, the toll of tiny cadavers would have been higher than the 110 that were reported in the press— perhaps much higher. Some bodies went undetected in the murky depths and others that were discovered would never reach the ears of journalists. Also, it was not unknown for a member of the public who stumbled across a child's cadaver to simply have it buried without telling the authorities—a turn of events that took place in the first instance in 1827 in the James Glen case below. Every discovery prompted questioning as to what sorry turn of events had preceded it, and a hunt for the mother would begin. Foul play was suspected in the majority of cases, as reflected in the headings "Supposed Infanticide", "Presumed Child Murder" and "A Suspicious Case". The phrase "Unnatural Murder" was also used, suggesting that the mother had failed to show the expected maternal instinct.

In many respects McNaughton's discovery followed the typical pattern. The majority of bodies were found by someone on the bank—a labourer in surrounding fields or an employee of industrial works en route to work. The newborn McNaughton found had been wrapped in brown paper, which was the material most frequently used for concealment since it was cheap and easy to come by. Also used were newspapers, cotton cloths, shawls or canvas bags; only two infants in separate cases were found in a wooden box. Nude cadavers were rare.

There was a good chance of getting away with it. The likelihood of identification and court proceedings following appears to have been less than fifty per cent. After McNaughton found the baby at Linlithgow, and the post-mortem showed death from asphyxia, Linlithgow Chief Constable Major E W Douglas issued a public appeal. The description of the pink dressing gown and basket was so detailed that Major Douglas must have been confident that a reader would recognise them as missing and come forward. But a year later the police were no closer to knowing who had left the boy in the hamper, and by then yet another anonymous infant had been found in the Union Canal. More children were reported found in the Union Canal than in any other Scottish waterway, with the majority in the Edinburgh area, and others in and around Falkirk and Linlithgow. Coming a close second was the Forth and Clyde, with discoveries clustering around the busy industrial areas of Port Dundas and Maryhill, and others at the Falkirk locks. However, every major Scottish canal has this unpleasant association, even the less populated Crinan and Aberdeenshire Canals.

In one-third of the newspaper reports there was good reason

to presume foul means: indications of violence before death were visible such as severe bruising to the head, skull fractures, gashes or slashes to the neck or signs of smothering. In three cases, a ribbon or rope was found tied about the neck. A post-mortem would be carried out to confirm the first impression. In some instances there were no obvious injuries and the physician would only commit to saying that the child had been born alive. Signs of asphyxia meant that death by drowning was thought probable, though the obstruction of breathing could have occurred earlier. On several occasions the act of ending the baby's life was witnessed by a lockkeeper or bridge-keeper, most conspicuously when the mother also attempted to drown herself. Only one case, in November 1849, was given the benefit of the doubt. An unidentified woman in her 30s was found drowned in the Union Canal with her baby at Butler's Bridge, Edinburgh. The Caledonian Mercury speculated that the mother might have been wandering the canal path in search of work and under cloud of night had stumbled and slipped into the water, though there was no firm evidence either way. In the great majority of cases where an examination was carried out, foul means were detected or suspected by the examining physician.

When passers-by saw something unusual around a canal they often feared it would be a child. In April 1833, rumours swept Ruchill in Glasgow that a missing child had been thrown in the Forth and Clyde, probably by the mother. The ensuing dragging operation failed to uncover the missing child, but uncovered the corpse of another child who had recently disappeared. Captain Alexander McCall, chief constable of the Glasgow police from 1870 to 1888, had to concede that scores of cases of found deceased children in the city were never investigated. Public awareness of the problem rose to a peak in the 1860s and it was reported more often. More than 23 children were found in canals in the 1860s, prompting letters demanding that action be taken. As the decade wore on the Glasgow courts handed out longer, harsher sentences often entailing penal servitude. The punitive approach had little effect, so the toll continued in the 1870s and 1880s. In January 1927, a group of schoolboys saw a couple carry a child along the bank of the Forth and Clyde at Bilsland Drive, Glasgow, only to notice a short time later that there was no sign of the child. Their reaction was to head straight for Maryhill police office, where their concern was taken seriously enough to launch a day-long dredging operation; no body was found.

In the cases that came to court, it was clear that these tragedies usually came about after the mother had tried to find support and was unsuccessful. Many women went looking for work, wandering between mills and manufactories with a babe-in-arms. In other cases, applications to the poorhouse, to family, friends and strangers and, of course, the child's father were rebuffed, as in the cases of Margaret McComb in 1827, Elizabeth Yates in 1847 and Elizabeth Keenan in 1863. The act often took place after it seemed that there was no possibility of food or shelter for the mother, and the effects of days, weeks or months of hunger and cold were setting in. Illegitimacy was also a consideration. An illegitimate birth would lead to the end of employment as a domestic servant or costs for someone to look after the child. In September 1856, Mary Wood tied a stone round her eleven-day-old baby girl and jumped after her into the Union Canal at Meggetland Bridge. She later confessed, saying: "It was because people would look down on me that I put the child in the water." In the Linlithgow Hamper Mystery it was noted that the umbilical cord was roughly cut, suggesting that the birth had taken place without proper medical intervention. The baby boy may well have been illegitimate.

Occasionally the act was attributed to psychological instability, or insanity as it was known. By 1860, thirty-seven year-old Elizabeth Paton had given birth to ten children, two of whom had died, and was in the lunatic ward of the poor house. She left the ward in the grip of a sort of religious mania in which she feared her children would literally be consumed by hellfire. She hoped to spare two of her children, Jamie aged three and Helen aged seven, by drowning them at Bridge 57 on the Union Canal, and following them herself. Helen managed to clamber out. Only three of the children abandoned in canals were known to have been left by men, in each case the father;

none was newborn. The first man had wanted rid of an illegitimate child. The other two had become widowers and descended into heavy drinking.

The establishment tended to attribute the phenomenon to a moral failing within the individual, despite the fact that there is no evidence of women wishing any harm on their children. The judiciary took a particularly harsh line in the first half of the nineteenth century, resting on the principles that wrongdoing mustn't go unpunished and the offence could be stamped out by making a painful example of the guilty. In sentencing the judge would direct a sermon to the prisoner, sometimes with a measure of fire and brimstone thrown in, though the woman's difficult circumstances were sometimes acknowledged. As for the general public, it is clear that a vein of sympathy for the mother ran through them. In the earlier nineteenth century when child murder was a hanging offence, juries always recommended mercy—in other words, they thought the woman's life should be spared and as a result a reprieve was generally granted. In 1847 public sympathy rose up for Elizabeth Yates, who drowned her son Murdoch McIntyre in the Union Canal, saying that as she held him under the water the child was already weak, and " ...she thought it best to put the child out of the world as she could not support it (him), and the father would not do so". The inhabitants of Glasgow called a public meeting to petition against the punishment of death. On receiving a letter from the Home Secretary, the Lord Provost hot-footed it to the prison to inform her of the news, though clearly in a poor psychological state, Yates showed no reaction.

When Georgina Love was found not proven by twelve votes to three for the culpable homicide of her baby in 1905, applause broke out in the court. Love did not fit the pattern of the child murderer. She was a happily married woman with two older children and a baby she loved. She was a known to be a quiet person who had developed a dependence on drink. After her brother refused to accompany her home to Govan, she made her way without money for food, but someone had given her whisky. She stopped by the Forth and Clyde, intending to wash her child's face. She testified that she hadn't known what she was doing owing to the drink and lack of food. Lord Ardwall told her that she must never drink again, for her misadventure had brought her near the gallows.

Newspaper reports show inconsistent moral attitudes and double-think. For example, the mother is described as destitute and hungry and simultaneously a calculating murderess. In 1903, twenty-two-year-old Margaret King was told that if she couldn't pay, the woman looking after her two-month-old son Thomas would no longer look after him. King said she had become demented and left her son by the side of a road, but he was found by two men passing by in the Union Canal. Though initially charged with murder by drowning, a plea of culpable homicide was accepted and the court was inclined to be lenient; the sentence was 18 months in prison. Unmarried and an inmate of the Falkirk poor house, King had supported herself from the age of twelve and became pregnant while working as a domestic servant. The *Falkirk Herald* heaped praise on the police for their ingenuity in unravelling the mysterious case while King, who wept bitterly throughout her trial, was described as "callous". In 1837 Ann Semple was charged with murdering her daughter Margaret close to the tunnel on the Paisley Canal and Lord Moncrieff sentenced her to execution. The *Caledonian Mercury* claimed that while Moncrieff was openly affected by the case Semple was unmoved and ate a sandwich with great enthusiasm; her hunger was taken as evidence of an unattractive character.

In 1862, a real-life scene worthy of the imagination of Dickens unfolded. Mary Scally was told by her father: "You shall not sit at this fireside with another man's child," and ordered her out into a snowstorm. Five months previously Scally had given birth to an illegitimate son whose father had gone away. In the Castlecary Murder, as it was known, the boy was found in the Forth and Clyde close to a bridge after having been suffocated or drowned. Her employer, Bothkennar farmer John Malcolm, described Scally as kind and obliging, an impression that was underlined by the local minister, and the court heard of her father's profound cruelty towards her. Throughout the trial Scally had cried and moaned as though in "intense mental agony". The court accepted the plea of culpable homicide and she was sentenced to three years penal servitude. The *Stonehaven Journal* reported that immediately following the act Scally had been overcome with remorse and tried to retrieve the child from the water. Yet the writer could not resist labelling her "callous".

It was seldom acknowledged that social conditions often lay behind this crime: that landlessness and insecure work created desperation, that wandering strangers or co-workers sometimes had to share a bed, and that some women unequipped with the facts of life then had to cope with the consequences in an atmosphere of overpowering shame. A few commentators showed awareness of this bigger picture. One letter writer to the *Scotsman* in 1864, 'Z D', was irate that a "wretch who had spent several years in corrupting and seducing young girls" received a relatively brief term of penal servitude. He contrasted the punishment of the hardened career criminal with the much harsher sentences handed down to young women who acted out of distress in the moment. Particularly moved by the case of Elizabeth Keenan below, Z D argued that well-educated women who were surrounded by parents, teachers and friends and what he called the thousand safeguards of society were unlikely to find themselves in the same desperate position. He suggested that unsupportive fathers should be punished also: "May it not be said that these poor women suffer for the sins of the people?"

The Distressing Case of Elizabeth Keenan

Brutal or callous treatment by the woman's husband, partner or father is a consistent feature of infanticide cases. The Lord Justice Clerk didn't think he had ever heard of such a distressing case as that of Elizabeth Keenan, a destitute woman who tried to drown herself and her five-week-old child, William, in the Paisley and Ardrossan Canal. The year was 1863. Her circumstances in the days and weeks before the incident, as described by witnesses in the courtroom, were so miserable that it is hard to imagine anything other than a sorry outcome. Keenan had been admitted to the lying-in hospital at

Rottenrow and on 30th June gave birth to William who, like his 2½ year-old-sister, was illegitimate. The father was William Ballantyne, of Anderston, who was in full-time employment as a maker of bolts and rivets. Three days later the mother and child left hospital and went to stay at the house of Jane McLeod in McAlpine Street, who had known Keenan for about six weeks.

After a couple of nights the Keenans went to Govan Poorhouse, but had to return five days later to McAlpine Street. McLeod allowed them to stay there so that Elizabeth could look for work, but three weeks later she hadn't found anything and was unable to contribute to their upkeep. McLeod believed Keenan was as attached to her baby as any mother could be, but she was clearly very poor and was suffering from hunger. At some point during this period, William Ballantyne came and spent one night sleeping on the floor at McLeod's place. He professed his fondness for the baby and promised to give Keenan some money when he got paid the following Friday. At the start of August McLeod told her lodger that she couldn't keep them any longer, since as she had children of her own to feed. She suggested that Keenan should apply to the fathers of her children; McLeod had once done so when in a similar position. Keenan asked McLeod to look after her older child till she came back. At nine o'clock at night she set off with the baby for Ballantyne's house. She met him outside the house and asked if he would help them. He refused. Since he was going to sleep at his sister's house she followed him, but there was a change of plan when he bumped into a friend, Edward Crawford. The pair took themselves to a public house, where Ballantyne bought himself some ale and told the pleading Keenan "go to hell".

Keenan was left with nowhere to go and nothing to eat, and slept with her infant on a common stair. The following day a sympathetic stranger gave her a cup of tea, her only nourishment that day, and the pair spent a second night on a stair. During the whole of the next day she did not even get a cup of tea. In the evening she had young William tied to her and wrapped inside a shawl. She set off along the banks of the Paisley and Ardrossan Canal in the direction of the Shields Bridge, walking very slowly and dabbing at the tears that flowed freely. A clerk named James McLean, passing with his friend Henry McFadyen, noticed her miserable condition. A short time later McLean saw that she had gone out of sight, and spotted a man on the parapet of the bridge who appeared to be listening for something. Then McLean heard the sound too—a woman screaming. He ran towards the bridge.

There was no sign of the woman he had seen crying, but something was visible in the water. The man on the parapet, William Fleming, had seen a dark object in the water, heard a choking sound and realised someone was shouting for help. A number of men from the vicinity then came together in a rescue attempt. They formed a human chain, each linking his hands to the other as they hauled the woman and child onto the bank. When both were safely out, the baby was handed to an elderly woman, Isabella Campbell, who saw him vomit a large quantity of water mixed with blood. Campbell feared that there could some kind of blockage in his chest. Meanwhile, Keenan began to come round and was asked if she taken drink. She explained that she'd had very little food and had thrown herself into the canal because she was weary of life. She asked for her child. Although young William appeared in a better condition than his mother, he wouldn't latch one and her attempts to nurse him were unsuccessful.

Mother and child were taken to the police office at Govan, to which Dr James Dunlop was summoned. On entering the room he could see that the woman was in a very feeble state and he doubted whether she was alive. He asked for her to be moved close to the fire, then turned his attention to the baby, who was conscious and crying out. Dunlop thought his pulse was good, his skin warm and breathing regular and he saw no obvious symptoms of asphyxia. Dunlop now examined Keenan. He found her skin cold and could detect no pulse. Applying his ear to her chest, however, he heard an indistinct noise and decided to attempt to revive her. This was a success and after a time it was decided to move them to the poor house. Dunlop arranged for Christian Wilson, poor house nurse, to look after the young William. Wilson had met the pair before during their earlier visit and was in no doubt as to Keenan's affection for her son. Wilson accompanied

Keenan and her child in a cab, ensuring both were well-wrapped in blankets. On arrival she was put to bed and Wilson administered two teaspoons of watery whisky toddy to both, according to the doctor's orders. As the night wore on baby William moaned and his breathing grew worse. The mother's attempts at feeding failed. Wilson clutched the boy to her bosom and he passed away. On the Friday of that week Keenan had a visitor. It was Jane McLeod, who found her former lodger very weak and ill.

Elizabeth Keenan was judged to be fit enough to stand trial in October of that year. She was charged with child murder and attempting to end her own life. The indictment said William Keenan had died the following day, 7th August, as a direct consequence of having been thrown with his mother into the canal. In her declaration she had stated it happened "while her head was turned with fatigue and privation," the father having refused to help her even though she was destitute. At the trial Jane McLeod attested to the mother's fondness for young William and related how Keenan had said that Ballantyne had promised money, but never gave her any. James McLean and the others involved in the rescue that night on the canal described their part in the drama. The court looked on with great interest at the most unsympathetic character in the room—the baby's father. Ballantyne claimed that on the evening when Keenan came to see him she hadn't seemed in want of food. He described how she had followed him and admitted that in response to her plea for help he had given her nothing but a few coppers. He owned up to having gone to buy ale with Edward Crawford, shortly after saying that he had no money. He suggested, disingenuously, that he didn't know for sure that the child was his, although he conceded there was no reason for thinking any other man could be the father. He denied having told her to go to hell. Keenan grew increasingly distressed as Ballantyne gave his contradictory evidence, and became distraught at any reference to the death of the young William.

Dr Dunlop was the first of three medical witnesses. Dunlop described observing in the baby no signs of asphyxia, which he understood to be a cause of drowning. He was aware that asphyxia could follow a pattern of unconsciousness, followed by rallying to wakefulness, then relapse. Surprisingly, he stated to the court that he could see no sign of starvation either, saying he saw nothing really wrong with the child. The other two medical witnesses, Drs Walter McKinlay and Samuel Moore, had examined young William's body. Neither had seen marks of violence on the boy. The court exchange with Dr McKinlay was complicated and protracted. He found that the death was caused by engorgement of his lungs, preventing the boy from breathing, and concluded that the engorgement was the result of asphyxia. However, there were inconsistencies. He averred that it was very rare someone taken out of the water to recover for a while and then pass away. Also, if the boy had cried out fully as Dunlop and Wilson had said, his lungs could not have been engorged at that point; it would not have been possible. Wilson had heard him cry as late as 3am, and a constable at the police office, Charles Stevenson, had heard him cry out like any baby separated for some time from his mother. Dr Moore agreed that the engorgement could only have taken place after the baby had ceased crying. His evidence took a third, slightly different tack, suggesting it was shock that had caused the boy's death.

Elizabeth Keenan's evidence would have melted the hardest heart. She described having pleaded with Ballantyne for money and how he had gone to into a public house in order to avoid her. She described the days of hanging around with nowhere to stay, relating that when she went into the canal… "I was tired of life and didn't know what I was doing." Suddenly proceedings came to an abrupt halt with the intervention of the advocate deputy. In light of the evidence heard he believed the case should be withdrawn for the consideration of the jury. Dr McKinlay's opinion that young William's death couldn't be connected directly with his submersion eleven hours before flew in the face of the evidence given by Dr Dunlop. He couldn't ask the jury to say that death resulted from the actions of the prisoner; they wouldn't be justified in convicting the prisoner on the charge. Looking at the circumstances, he believed it was his duty to relieve the jury of the painful duty they would have had to carry out with regard to Keenan's guilt.

The Lord Justice Clerk wholeheartedly agreed. The medical evidence, he said, had failed to establish that the death of the child was a result of his submersion in the canal. The jury then formally returned the verdict of not guilty, news that was received with a spontaneous burst of applause from all who were looking on. The judge, not kindly disposed to this expression of emotion in the court, quickly suppressed it. A collection was then taken by Keenan's defence in the courtroom so that she would have some money to live off after her discharge. About fifty shillings was collected and handed to her. Whether Keenan managed to find some means of subsistence for herself and her older child in the longer term is not clear. The *Glasgow Daily Herald* of October 7th, 1863, reported on the case and, noting that four cases of infanticide that had come to court in recent days, observed: "This brutal neglect by men who have ruined young women is not rare."

The Beggar Woman at the Cross

He was found at the New Plash, a basin of the Forth and Clyde Canal about three miles from Glasgow: a fair-haired baby boy no more than a year and a half old, dressed in blue flannel, a linen pinafore, a cotton shift. His feet were bare and he was covered in mud. He was found lifeless in the water and must have been there for some time. The process of putrefaction was beginning to turn the skin of his face and body to a greenish hue. Flowing from his mouth was a frothy-looking liquid and his throat bore a distinctive furrow with a ridged edges. The backs of his legs were darkened in two places by what appeared to be burns.

The man who made the grim discovery on a May morning in 1827 was John Johnston, who lived at Ruchill drawbridge on the Forth and Clyde Canal. He was out at 5 o'clock in the morning when he saw the child's body floating on the water and fished it out. He was joined by another man, James Corbett, and later a woman arrived who appeared to be the mother; she took the child's clothing. Within hours the tiny body had been put into a coffin and Corbett, Johnston and the mother attended an informal burial at Maryhill churchyard.

That rather hasty funeral might have been the end of it, had the police not been informed of the turn of events. The following day two medics, Dr Corkindale and Dr Nielsen, were sent to perform the task of disinterring the body for examination. At the graveside was the mother, who identified the child as hers. Johnson and Corbett also attended in order to identify this as the mud-coated child they found floating in the water. In their subsequent report, the physicians said the boy was unlikely to have died of a disease, as he had probably appeared healthy in life. They noted the marks on the legs that looked like burns, and the impression over the windpipe. Though they couldn't be certain that strangulation had been the cause of death, the child had suffered a hand or a piece of string tight about his neck.

The child was now identified as James Glen, his mother as Margaret McComb and his father a carter of the same name as his son, who had grown up in Bearsden. The police wanted a word with the carter. The same day as the medical examination Constable John Geddes and a colleague spotted him driving his cart, which was empty, towards the canal. He was a good-looking man of only twenty-two years of age, shorter than average and of slender build. Geddes seized Glen's horse by the head and ordered him to climb down. "What for?" was the reply. After a short display of defiance from the carter, the constables pulled him down.

James Glen Senior was taken to the police station. He acknowledged that he was the father of the child and made two declarations in which he protested his innocence. His circumstances were not conducive to family life. Ill health had left him without work or money, so he was reduced to relying on the hospitality of friends, the More family, to provide a roof over his head. He had not drowned his son; on the contrary, he had sought to give young James a fresh start by finding someone who could look after him. He had in mind a Mrs Adams who ran a lodging house in the Gallowgate. He set out one evening with the boy and the sum of 12 shillings in his pocket, which the

Mores had given him. But before reaching the Gallowgate, he met a beggar woman who agreed take the child off his hands. Though the woman was a stranger to him, he handed the child over to her charge. She was elderly, spoke with a Scottish accent and wrapped in a brown coat. That was the only description Glen could give the police of the woman he'd given charge of his son.

The version of events given by Margaret McComb was somewhat less heartening, and featured no flourishes such as a mystery beggar woman. McComb had become pregnant by Glen when he was staying in her father's house and gave birth to a baby boy in January 1826. James junior had been a healthy child apart from burns to the legs that were sustained when he got too close to the fire. When the boy reached about six months, Glen had given McComb £2 to assist with looking after him, a sum that lasted until the Spring of 1827, when McComb went to the More's house to ask Glen for more money. Glen said he had none, but promised to meet her at Glasgow Cross the following Monday night. She went to the Cross and waited until 10 o'clock at night, but there was no sign of Glenn. On the Tuesday afternoon she went to him at the More's house, where mother and child did not exactly receive a warm welcome. "What the hell do you want?" was the father's greeting. He told her to go back to where she came from, as he had no money. McComb said she would leave the child with him, to which he replied, "If you leave the thing here, I'll drown it before two hours." McComb though he was saying this only to frighten her, and left the boy at the More's house.

The mother returned to the More's house on the Sunday, but there was no sign of her baby. Glen laughed at her and said he would never tell. She said she would never fash (trouble) him again—she would beg bread from people's doors first—if only he would give her the child. At this, he flew at her and seized her by the throat. She grabbed a poker, which he snatched back. He didn't hit her with it, but he knocked her down using his hands and a shouting match ensued, in which McComb asked Mrs More why on earth they allowed such an awful man under their roof. Shortly after McComb strode out of the

More's house, she heard that a child had been found drowned in the canal at Ruchill draw bridge. She walked the two miles there and on seeing the clothes and hair, immediately recognised her son.

The police were inclined to believe McComb's account. After being apprehended by Constable Geddes, James Glen was imprisoned in the Glasgow jail with a number of other prisoners. But before the trial for infanticide could take place, a drama erupted at the prison. On evening of Saturday, 2nd June, the prisoners were locked up as usual, Glen in a cell with one other man. Five of the jail's residents had been convicted at the assizes and were due for transportation to the other side of the world. Another four, like Glen, were awaiting trial, although for less serious offences such as theft.

On the Sunday morning the turnkeys unlocked the door as usual just before 8 o'clock and let the ten prisoners spill out into the day room. While they waited unsupervised for breakfast to arrive, the prisoners began to execute what appeared to be a well-made plan, probably devised by the five convicts who had nothing to lose. They tore a hinge off the wall and door of the toilet, then used the hinge to free an iron panel that covered the lock on one of the cells. This enabled them to force open the door to the lobby. The ten spilled out onto the stair where they remained in a silent huddle. When the unsuspecting turnkeys appeared with breakfast, the prisoners ambushed and struck out the iron panel, the hinge and a lead pipe someone had torn from the water closet. Leaving the jailers wounded and bruised on the floor, they surged towards the door, knocking down the doorkeeper on their rush towards freedom.

Eight of the men ran up Market Lane and into King Street, two of them armed. The other two crossed a wooden bridge. The experience of breaking prison must have been exhilarating for James Glen. But he was accused of infanticide, the most serious sort of crime that could be conceived of. He could get no rest, running from place to place. The harsh reality of life on the run soon caught up with him, so within two days he was handing himself in at the jail door.

At the trial in November 1827, Mrs More was able to confirm that

McComb had indeed left the child at her house and expanded on the unhappy scene. An almighty war of words had broken out, she said, in which obscenities that upset her were used, Glen had threatened to drown the boy, and McComb swore that she would hunt him to the gallows. More revealed that she had offered to look after the child, but Glen declined, saying she had plenty of children of her own. More then offered to keep the child for the night, but Glen took the boy away between eight and nine, saying he would give him to an acquaintance. As he went, More slipped a shawl over his shoulders to keep him warm. When Glen returned the next day McComb didn't notice any change in his mood, though he had acquired a new shirt while in Glasgow. Under cross examination, she gave a description of the lad that was at odds with what the court had just heard. He was, she said, a sober and steady lad of gentle disposition.

John Geddes, the special constable who apprehended Glen, also appeared as a witness. He said that when they pulled Glen off his cart, he had protested with the words: "I'm innocent—it wasn't me that drowned the child." Geddes believed that this betrayed Glen's involvement, for neither police officer had told him that they were investigating the drowning of a child. However, it was possible he had heard this some other way. The physicians' evidence was heard, and Glen's legal representative argued that there was not enough evidence to prove the charge.

The Lord Advocate said he believed the case had involved no common degree of criminality and sent the jury away. After ten minutes they returned the verdict of guilty. The Lord Justice Clerk said that as there was no crime of a more black or atrocious nature, Glen must abandon hope for mercy and sentenced him to death by hanging. At the jail, Glen was fed on bread and water and was seen to undertake his spiritual preparations for the hereafter seriously. He made a confession in which he claimed that he had not strangled his son but, acting under the influence of the devil, had thrown on the canal when he was asleep. The execution took place before a large crowd on 12th December. After hanging as an example to all for forty-five minutes, the body was lowered into a coffin at the foot of the scaffold. A carter then took the body to be dissected by Dr James Jeffray, Professor of Anatomy at the University of Glasgow. The carter thereafter found himself and his horse attacked by a large, bloodthirsty mob.

The James Glen case is unusual for the father being the perpetrator. In two other cases where the father was responsible for the infanticide, the mother had died and the act was part of a suicide attempt. Retired spirit dealer Hugh McLaughlin of Port Dundas had sunk into alcoholism and depression following his wife's death; he jumped into the canal with his daughter in 1896. Only four years later, widower James Dougall, a 29-year-old butcher, was sent to prison for nine months after jumping in the Forth and Clyde with his son, John.

A Sham Marriage

In the early twentieth century, some women were still living in appalling circumstances. In February 1923, Mary Blaney took her one-year-old baby girl in her arms and headed from Carnbroe towards the Monkland Canal, saying she was going for a walk. That wasn't true. Mary had reached the end of her tether and all she could think of was ending it all with her baby. She reached the bridge at Brewsterford and tried to squeeze herself through the railings. As she did so the baby slipped out of her hands and into the water. The sudden splash brought her to her senses. She leaned through the railings and managed to grab one of the baby's feet, but the girl's sock came off and Mary could only watch as her girl sank into the dank, deep canal. The next twenty-four-hours were a blur—Mary would later recall nothing of it. She began wandering absently and was discovered the next day shouting out that her child had drowned. When the details of what had happened became known, she was arrested and imprisoned.

Mary was only twenty years old and earned 24 shillings a week at a brick works. One of nine children, she had endured a life of extraordinarily cruel treatment by her family, which was now laid before the courts. At first she appeared at the Sherriff Court, but was referred to the High Court. Mr Sandeman, appearing on Mary's behalf, said that for years her alcoholic parents had taken all her wages and she lived in destitution. When she was only fifteen she was introduced to a thirty-year-old man who was her mother's cousin. The man asked her to accompany him to Glasgow one day, where Mary was asked to sign something she didn't understand. She had been tricked into marriage. The con marriage was never consummated, as the motivation that lay behind it was financial. Her mother received an allowance for the husband's absence, as he was a soldier, and not a penny of it was given to Mary.

Things looked more positive to Mary when she met a man whose surname was Kelly and the couple fell in love. Mary was expecting a baby and they planned to wed. On the appointed day of the wedding, Mary's legal husband appeared and claimed that she was already married to him. Mr Kelly made himself scarce, and so the young woman was bringing up the baby on her own. She then met a second man, by the name of McLean, who proposed to her. Since Mary didn't believe that she could really be married already, she went ahead with the plans. The date was set for February 17th. In the weeks before the wedding McLean bought clothes for his intended family and some furniture, all of it kept at the house where Mary and her daughter still lived with her parents. Four days before the wedding Mary arrived home to find that her parents' cruelty towards her had surpassed itself. They pair, utterly intoxicated, shouted a volley of taunts and abuse at her. This bout of drinking they had funded by selling all the clothes and furniture McLean had bought—every last stitch and stick of it.

Lord Ormidale said he had listened carefully and he accepted that the painful life Mary had led played its part in leading to the tragic drowning. However, it was a serious charge, he said, and he was keeping in mind that she had thought to end the child's life with her own. He imposed a sentence of twelve months' imprisonment.

Mary left the dock crying bitterly. The justice system had done her no favours. Her parents, who had stolen from her for years and manipulated her into a sham marriage, should have been in the dock. To compound the insult, Ormidale seems not to have heeded that the distraught woman hadn't known what was doing that night on the bridge at Brewsterford.

1. Port Dundas, 1950s. For decades, homeless young men like John Broadfoot sought warmth and shelter amid the industrial premises on the Forth and Clyde Canal.

2. Euphemia Bourhill was found dead by the Causewayend Bridge on the Union Canal following a savage attack.

FIFTY POUNDS REWARD.

2 4 5

MURDER.

THE BODY of a WOMAN, evidently MURDERED,
having been found in the Edinburgh and Glasgow Union
Canal, near Causewayend, in the County of Stirling, on the
2d of November 1847, and having been identified as the body
of a Dealer in Fruit and Cakes, named EUPHEMIA BOUR-
HILL, last seen on the night of the 15th of October 1847, on
her way from Mid Calder Fair to Edinburgh, and believed to
have been Murdered on the Night of the 15th or Morning of
the 16th October 1847, between Keirshill Toll Bar and Burnwynd, in the County of Edinburgh.

A REWARD OF FIFTY POUNDS STERLING
is hereby offered to any Person who shall give such information to the PROCURATOR-FISCAL of the County of Edinburgh, at the County Buildings, Lawnmarket, Edinburgh, as
shall lead to the discovery of material circumstances connected
with the Removal of the Body from Keirshill Toll Bar, or Dal-
mahoy Gate, or Burnwynd, or any part of the road between or
near these places, to the Canal.

Edinburgh, 27th Nov. 1847.

3. Six weeks after Euphemia Bourhill's murder, this reward notice offering £50 for information was published in the *Caledonian Mercury*.

4. Explosives expert Colonel Majendie was brought in to investigate the bomb plot at Possil Road Aqueduct in 1883.

5. The Forth and Clyde Canal at Maryhill, 1935. Dredging operations were carried out in this area following suspicious reports of missing children in 1833.

6. At the northern end of the Caledonian Canal, lock-keeper's daughter Marjory Mackintosh was attacked by a local farmer.

7. The Kintore murder. Illustration depicting the moment Ann Forbes was lured into Thainstone plantation by wood merchant George Stephen.

THEY WENT INTO THE PLANTATION.

8. The Inn at Ratho where notorious canal murderer George Bryce lived. He set off across the bridge in search of his victim.

9. Artist's depiction of Bryce's vengeful assault on nursemaid Jeannie Seaton.

HE CUT HER THROAT.

10. Edinburgh surgeon Dr Joseph Bell, said to have been the inspiration for Sherlock Holmes, appeared as an expert witness at the trial of James Munn.

11. Ambitious canal clerk Captain Cheyne mixed with the grandees of the Linlithgow and Stirlingshire Hunt.

12. Hillside at Preston Fields above the Union Canal, where Captain Cheyne shirked his duties to ride with the hounds.

13. Union Canal engineer Hugh Baird suffered financially after Cheyne tightened his grip on the company finances.

14. The Gorbals parish records the death from hanging of 25-year-old Bell McMenemy.

1828		Names	Male	Female	Disease	181
Oct	21	Mary Anderson	38	39 78	Age	
"		Mary McDonald		12	Water kind	
"		Mary Tuck		6 m	S. pox	
"		Alexr Cunningham	2 m°		Bowel Complt	
"		Mary Ann Donachie		13 m°	Con	
"		Still Born female		0		
"	22	Robt Dennot	2		Water kind	
"		Sarah Callum		12	Con	
"		Still Born male	0			
"		Do Do female		0		
"	23	Isabel McMenemy		25	Hanged	

CHAPTER FOUR: WOMEN BEWARE

The Ghost of Black Wood

Given the passing of time, a notorious crime can come to be associated with the menace of the supernatural. This particularly applies to crimes of a macabre and brutal nature that have taken place in an evocative setting. One hauntingly lonely spot on the Crinan Canal rose to infamy in the early nineteenth century following a disturbing turn of events. At this time the landscape felt very remote. The traveller going west from Lochgilphead would leave behind the attractive Auchindarroch Farm and Estate and head into terrain that increasingly grew boggy and barren. Beyond a left turn where a contractor once tried to cut a direct path through the moss, the traveller would take a lengthy path by the edge of the Black Wood, so called because of its gloomy aspect. With the next farm, Craig Glass, some way off, not a single dwelling would be in sight across moor and hill. Beyond the Black Wood a broken-down bridge crossed a stream, and it was above the water that the traveller might experience a shiver down the spine. In 1804, this place was the scene of a chilling incident that left ghostly whispers behind.

Though this corner of Argyll was no hotspot for serious crime, it was regarded as a little backwards and lawless. During their time ashore the fishermen would gather to drink, carouse and generally disturb the sober folk. The local youth was also a problem. Unpleasant scuffles would break out at Lochgilphead market, in which drunken young men from the different parishes squared up to one another using any sticks and branches they could find. One man who stayed away from these affrays was Duncan MacArthur, who lived by the locks at Cairnbaan. MacArthur was socially on the fringe as he was commonly regarded as a sort of village idiot. A glimmer of happiness came along for him in the shape of a woman named Elizabeth McKinnon, whom he courted and later married. However, Mrs MacArthur's appearance drew attention of the unwelcome sort. She was judged to be no beauty and a group of local young stirrers began to direct a stream of derogatory remarks her way. To make matters worse the MacArthurs failed to produce the expected offspring, offering the wagging tongues more material for malicious gossip. As the campaign of taunts against his wife went on, MacArthur's mental health deteriorated and he yearned for a way out. In time he thought up a plan. It was drastic, but sure to bring the intimidation to an end. Perhaps he could see no other way out.

One day he persuaded Elizabeth to accompany him along the west bank of the canal. As they reached the rickety bridge at Black Wood he had a quick glance about to make sure the coast was clear, then shoved her into the water. The desperate woman made a grab for a small willow bush overhanging the water, all the time crying out for mercy—in vain, as MacArthur's mind was made up. He uprooted a fence post and beat her about the head until she slipped into the water and drowned. At this point MacArthur realised he had a new problem, and took to his heels. His disappearance underlined the suspicions that he had finished off his wife. It wasn't long till he was captured. The first attempt to bring the case to court in April 1804 had to be postponed for the lack of a witness. Rumour had it that two men had been on the opposite bank during the drowning and had tried unsuccessfully to intervene, but they were thought to be visitors and couldn't be identified. Finally, in September of that year, the trial went ahead based on circumstantial evidence. MacArthur decided to make a confession, and the jury duly came to a guilty verdict. The judge sentenced him to be hanged on 31st October on the spot where he had taken his wife's life. As a posthumous punishment MacArthur's body was to be taken to Inverary and given to surgeon John Anderson for dissection.

On the morning of the hanging Lochgilphead became a scene of unwonted bustle. Shopkeepers left their premises and fishing boats were brought ashore. Men, women and children spilled out of their homes to join a crowd moving in drifts along the canal. They gathered in front of a huge wooden apparatus on the banks, the likes of which had never been seen in the district before. The sturdy gallows had partly been financed by donations from local landowners who hoped, like the judiciary, that making an example of MacArthur would deter any like-minded man from doing away with his wife. Most chillingly, it stood opposite the house of the murderer. When his moment came, the condemned man spoke to the crowd and expressed his acceptance that justice had been done. The body was then sent to Inverary, but the anatomisation was never carried out. It was returned to MacArthur's parents for burial after Dr Anderson refused to accept it. Perhaps the surgeon had known the family or was afraid of making himself unpopular. Whatever the reason for the doctor's actions, that would not be the end of it.

Before long the locals began to see things. Just a month after the murder two men travelling in the moonlight to Lochgilphead came to the bend in the canal where the murder had taken place. They were horrified to see something glinting white on the water that could be the ghost of the dying woman. They hastily turned back to the Cairnbaan Inn, then owned by a man named Neil. They blurted out what they had seen while Neil had to calm them down with some old-fashioned hospitality. Then, on another moonlit night at the turn of the year, the owner of Walkingdon Farm was returning with a friend from an early-evening expedition to Knapdale. There was an eerie but picturesque chill in the air. Having decided to walk the final stretch, the pair handed their horses to a groom who went on ahead. As they reached the fatal spot they were already talking about the legend of the ghost and there it was, a white figure looming over the water. One of the pair gamely resolved that he would approach the spectre. His companion, against his better judgement, followed. At close quarters they could see that they had been spoked by; it was nothing more than an old birch tree with silvery white bark. Once they were back in the safety of the farmhouse they could laugh at it. The oldest people in the nearby villages, however, were slower to make light of it. They knew that no one else had been hanged thereabouts in living memory, and believed that the association with Duncan McArthur's deeds was certain to linger.

Strife on Water Street

The year was 1894, and George Hannah was working as a private watchman on the north side of the Forth and Clyde in the Port Dundas area. At about ten o'clock one Saturday night in October he heard distress cries of "Murder!" and "Police!" on the south bank close to Spier's Wharf. This was followed by a splash and the sound of someone struggling. He then heard a man's voice say: "Kate, come here and catch this." Hannah rushed to the spot, which was close to a bridge. Though he could see nobody in trouble in the water, he caught sight of a man who was running away from the scene. An unnamed passer-by told him that a woman had been in the water, but she was now out of sight. Hannah asked the passer-by to wait there while he went to summon the nearest bridge-keeper for assistance. A short time later, watchman and bridge-keeper were looking up and down the water for signs of life, but to no avail. All they could do was inform the police of what had happened.

Several officers arrived at the scene with their standard canal-searching implements, grappling irons. At about two o'clock in the morning their search came to an unhappy conclusion with the discovery of a woman's body. It wasn't long before a man was able to identify the deceased as his missing sister-in-law, Catherine Murphy or Dundon. The 26-year-old woman had lived in a thoroughfare named Water Street, a name that seemed with the benefit of hindsight rather ill-fated. The street, which was later re-named, ran towards the canal. Murphy's brother-in-law was also able to point the police towards a suspect, an individual who had been hanging around Murphy in recent weeks.

William Barton, a 30-year-old mason who came originally from Dumfries, was in custody by the Sunday evening. At the Northern Police Court he admitted he had been "keeping company" with Murphy for some time and had been with her on the Saturday night in question. He then went on to give a questionable explanation for what had happened. He had been walking with her along Water Street at ten o'clock on the Saturday night. Murphy had suddenly run away from him in the direction of the canal bank and at the bridge she had thrown herself into the water, where she drowned. He was kept in custody and the case was remitted to the sheriff while further investigations went on. It was incriminating that the cries of "Murder!" had been heard and a man close to Barton's description was seen fleeing the scene of the drowning. However, it appears that the prosecution of Barton petered out, since the records fall silent. Presumably the Sheriff had taken the view that there was insufficient evidence to prove that he had pushed Murphy into the water.

Canalside Assaults

The linear environment of a canal towpath presents opportunities to individuals looking to mount a surprise attack on a passing woman. Sheds and other buildings lining the towpath enhance these opportunities by providing an effective place for the perpetrator to lurk and take the advantage of surprise. The route may be hidden from public view and the lone walker may abruptly pass from a busy, overlooked zone to a quiet stretch where there is no one around. Manmade structures can provide cover for an attack in the shape of shadowy recesses at or beneath bridges or, as in one incident described below, natural features such as shrubs and woodlands can be used by the perpetrator to facilitate an ambush or escape.

With some of the attacks on women, the motive is elusive. It may be that a sexual element was expunged from the newspaper accounts in order to preserve the good name of the victim. In the following cases the women seem simply to have been passers-by. No motive was reported for an attack on Christmas Eve, 1889 on a woman named Margaret McCormack as she made her way along a quiet section of the towpath of the Union Canal at Broxburn. Out of the blue a man grabbed her by the hair, knocked her down and kicked her. He was subsequently identified as miner John Brannan and was sent to prison for 60 days. Likewise, no reason was given for an incident in 1939. A clerkess named Edith Hankinson suffered an unprovoked attack while walking alongside the locks of the Forth and Clyde with her sister's two children. At Lock 16, a man appeared seemingly from nowhere and struck her on the shoulder with his fist. At the Police Court in Falkirk, James Sinclair at first tried to maintain his innocence, but later changed his plea to guilty. The punishment was imposed of 15 shillings or ten days' imprisonment.

One widely-reported assault on a young girl in July 1950 on the Forth and Clyde could have had fatal consequences. The attacker concealed himself on the fringe of a wood at Cadder, Lanarkshire. Sixteen-year-old Rae Tennent, of Bishopbriggs, was walking past a clump of bushes when the man ran out and struck her on the side of the head with a lemonade bottle. The dazed schoolgirl staggered back and grappled with the man, and in the tussle both ended up in the canal. A struggled ensued in the water before the man clambered out. Bizarrely, he offered to help his victim climb out of the canal before making off. A strong swimmer, Tennent went managed to fetch a shoe she had lost in the water and was helped out by two cyclists who had heard her screams. While she dried off in the safety of a nearby house the cyclists went into the wood after the assailant. It was the following morning that the man was arrested and the case came to court at the start of August. Thirty-year-old Springburn man Thomas Mure Kelly pleaded guilty to assaulting the schoolgirl. The punishment was a fine of £60 with the option of 60 days imprisonment, a remarkably lenient sentence given that a poorer swimmer could easily have drowned.

It is difficult to glean much insight into the historical phenomenon of canalside rape. Reports of rapes, indecent assault and exposure alongside canals are far more numerous in the present-day media than in newspapers during the historical period covered by this book. Yet there is no reason for thinking that these things were rarer then. It is more likely that sensibilities would have discouraged victims from reporting incidents to the police. The sexual dimension of life was seldom acknowledged by the mainstream (which is why prostitution on boats and on the banks during this period proves extremely difficult to chronicle). In many nineteenth-century cases where charges such as libidinous practices were reported the location is not revealed. To make matters even more opaque, the earlier cases were heard behind closed doors, leaving most of the details obscure.

One notorious canalside rape, condemned by judge Lord Meadowbank as "deplorable", occurred in 1841 on the Caledonian Canal. The victim was 13-year-old Marjory MacIntosh, known as May. Alexander McRae attacked her at a spot between Dochgarroch and Bught Bridge. The trial at Edinburgh's High Court was held up after the Inverness mail coach, on which several witnesses were travelling, got caught in a storm. As the evidence was led behind closed doors little is recorded about the turn of events. The victim, who may have been suffering from TB, was the daughter of lock-keeper Donald McIntosh. Her assailant was fifty-year-old McRae, a local farmer and cattle dealer. Pronouncing sentence, Meadowbank donned the black cap and ordered McRae to be taken under secure guard to Inverness to be hanged at the place of his crime. Clearly disgusted by the crime, the judge stated that he could see no vestige of a ground that would justify sparing MacRae the hangman's rope.

Even though the jury agreed, and didn't recommend him to mercy, McRae was given a reprieve. With 307 other convicts who mostly came from England and Ireland, McRae was forced to board the David Clarke for a four-month journey to Van Diemens Land, now Tasmania. He would face penal servitude for life. Marjory McIntosh was by no means the only young girl to be targeted in a canalside rape. An eleven-year-old, Williamina Smith, was attacked by a man ten years older. William Milliken received five years' imprisonment for this rape on the banks of the Forth and Clyde in 1901. In 1944, twelve-year-old Agnes Lawrie of Abercorn was approached and terrified by a man on the bank of the Union Canal. Adam Johnston was sentenced to 12 months for assault and lewd practices with intent to rape.

Death of a Weelwisher

The following case shows how violent crime can be tied to changes in wider economic circumstances. The Aberdeenshire Canal came to Inverurie just after the turn of the nineteenth century, and the settlement of Port Elphinstone developed as its bustling inland depot. A long-standing resident of Port Elphinstone was cartwright George Stephen, an unmarried 62-year-old who supported his mother and two nieces. Like other local tradesmen he benefited from his proximity to the waterway. In the late 1840s, business was brisk and he sought an apprentice. However, the canal was failing to turn a profit.

Parts of the canal route were snapped up by the Great North of Scotland Railway and within ten years the infrastructure of iron and steam had arrived on Stephen's doorstep. Rails were laid from Port Elphinstone to Huntly and later to Aberdeen, leaving only vestiges of the canal. In these changed circumstances, there were winners and losers. Trade in grain and manure went on apace and a paper mill was established. However, the Port Elphinstone Inn and a bone-grinding facility shut down. Stephen's workshop saw a steady downturn and by the early 1860s his sales of timber, ladders and other wooden goods were dwindling. The bankruptcy of a nephew in 1862 was a further blow, costing him hundreds of pounds, and rising rent demands weighed on him. Stephen's descent into financial anxiety would culminate in tragedy.

It was a Saturday afternoon in December 1864. Just after lunch a small party braved the cold to hunt game in Thainston Woods. Among the party were the owner of Thainston Lodge, Bell Fisher, and his coachman George Campbell Shepherd. Out in front, acting as beater, was fourteen-year-old John Cruickshank, son of the estate gardener. A short distance from the road Cruickshank entered a secluded alcove encircled by trees and glimpsed something on the forest floor. It was a woman lying face down. Shepherd, shouting from further away, suggested she might be drunk, but a closer look left no room for doubt. Blood flowed from a large wound to the back of her head. A blow from some sort of heavy weapon had driven the red flannel she wore into the fracture. She had been subjected to a savage attack that left her unable to tell what had happened. Shepherd set off in a cart to fetch a doctor. He also alerted the police at Inverurie and at Kintore, a mile to the south.

The hunting party was joined by Mary Milne, keeper of the

porter's lodge nearby. Milne identified the woman as Ann Forbes, an inhabitant of Aberdeen who was known to visit Port Elphinstone regularly. She was dressed in the garb of the destitute: a petticoat, a well-worn gown, a shawl, shabby galoshes and the red flannel that served as a poor substitute for a bonnet; it would later emerge that these rags had been borrowed. Kintore surgeon Alex Irvine arrived and after a brief examination of the patient had her moved to the porter's lodge. Despite his ministrations, little could be done in the wake of such a savage attack.

Three policemen arrived at the scene, Inspectors Aiken and Wyness, and Constable Henry. They seized a note tucked into Forbes' shawl. Although the paper inside was blank, the address on the outside led them to the door of George Stephen. Although a search of the house revealed little, the workshop turned up axes. One drew attention with its blood-like stains. Aiken rifled through a trunk and a drawer, seeking clues in letters and papers. A possible motive emerged in a letter that had been written three months previously, which the unfortunate woman had signed: "your weelwisher, Ann Forbes". It was an outpouring referring to a long-standing friendship that had clearly been a great deal more than that. In this and other letters Forbes was pressing Stephen to meet her and asking him for money. Forbes suggested that the potentially scandalous friendship might be exposed by her, or by one of Stephen's relatives. One note set out the arrangements for the fatal meeting that Saturday, with Forbes emphasising that she had "something very particular to say" and urging Stephen not to leave her waiting. There could be no doubt that she was putting him under pressure. Could the motive for the murder be blackmail? By five o'clock George Stephen had been apprehended.

The crime was sufficiently serious that an eminent medical man was called in. Dr Ogston, Professor of Medical Jurisprudence at Aberdeen University, joined Dr Irvine. They examined the site in the clearing and ruled out the possibility of the injury being caused by falling on a tree stump. A small indentation saturated with blood was the main trace left by the incident. The lack of evidence of a struggle led Ogston to the conclusion that a heavy blow had been landed from behind. Examining the patient at the lodge, he noted two wounds to the head, one four inches long. The procurator fiscal also attended, just in case Forbes could manage to make a statement. Mary Milne stayed with Forbes all afternoon and evening. She was unable to utter a word, and no one was surprised when she passed away at 8pm. This was now a murder inquiry.

Information gathered about Mrs Forbes made for a sorry tale that had made a happy ending unlikely. She was about 50 years of age and lived at Gordon's Court, Virginia Street, Aberdeen. Her second husband William was 64-year-old former shoemaker who had become bedbound and utterly dependent on her. The couple got eight shillings per month from the city parochial board, which Forbes supplemented with odd jobs such as doing laundry. The week before her death she had called in at the board medical office, requesting help, which suggests her desperation may have been worsening. Both the funeral and burial at Kintore churchyard were paid for from the parish poor fund. The chief mourner was her seaman brother.

Stephen was taken to Aberdeen on the Sunday to give his declaration before the sheriff. In a cool, calm voice he declared he had never known the victim in life, and nor did he recognise her in death. There had, however, been too many witnesses to the secret meetings between Forbes and Stephen. Gossip abounded that Forbes had had an illegitimate child by George Stephen, but the medics quashed this; their examinations convinced them that this was a woman who had never given birth. In the days following the murder, column inches throughout the country were given to The Kintore Murder, with speculation as to potential blackmail and the dramatic decline in Stephen's physical and mental condition.

At the trial in April 1865, questions over Stephen's sanity were raised from the outset. The prisoner surprised all present, including his own counsel, by pleading guilty to the murder charge. Sheriff Watson asked for the full facts to be heard, since a special plea had been entered that Stephen had been insane when he committed the act. As regarded the violence that took place in the wood that day, little was left to the imagination as the medics gave their testimonies. Irvine described his removal of blood, hair and twenty fragments of bone from the wound. Ogston had examined the axe under a microscope and found evidence of gravel and vegetation from the woodland, fibres from the red head-flannel and, of course, blood. Both medical men had spoken to Stephen after he was apprehended and found him morose.

The witnesses who knew Stephen told a story of a formerly mild man who had changed following an illness about three months before the incident. Port Elphinstone postmaster John Thomson noted a strange look in his eye and related an odd conversation in which the wood merchant claimed he had no fire to cook with although the fire was in front of him; he also said inaccurately that, thanks to his financial woes, he had no food to eat and his bed was a cairn of stones. Thomson thought the disturbance in his mind been triggered by financial worries. Stephen had become obsessed with the dread of becoming bankrupt. In detail, his nieces described a series of epileptic fits that became obvious in the August of that year. He had bitten his tongue, affecting his speech in the long term. Axes were very much a tool of Stephen's trade. His mother attributed this to his work life as a sawyer but in the light of events his habit of carrying an axe behind his back had taken on a darker significance. Jane Duncan had seen him disappear into Thainston Woods after Ann Forbes several times. On the 3rd of December he followed her with an axe at his back.

The letters, including the weelwisher note, formed a key part of the evidence. It emerged that Forbes had been illiterate, and the letters were written by a woman named Eliza Pyper. Pyper was one of three Aberdeen women who, as neighbours of the victim, could shed some light on her destitute and shadowy existence. Forbes had a reputation. She had been seen taking drink in the company of a seaman. Over the years she had visits from George Stephen at home and as if to justify it she had put about a story that he gave her money to support a child. However, there had never been any sign of a child. On the morning of the murder, the pettitcoat and shawl Forbes was found in had been lent to her by one of the neighbours, a Margaret Thomson.

The declaration Stephen had made on the day of the murder was read out. Before Sheriff Watson he had uttered an outright denial that he had ever known Forbes. The defence suggested that he was of unsound mind resulting from "a morbid dread of want". A tailor he had long known, William Bruce, noted his anxiety over money peaking about two weeks before the epileptic fits began, when he talked as if he had neither food nor fuel, although he had both. One day Stephen had called five times Bruce's place and was inconsolable over his financial circumstances. After the fits, Bruce considered that he had lost his wits. Several witnesses, including Stephen's mother, testified that as his health deteriorated he became child-like and said very little. Two local doctors spoke of visits to Stephen, with one offering the view that disease had weakened his mind.

The jury was only twenty minutes in finding Stephen guilty. There had never been any doubt that he administered the fatal blows and the special plea of insanity hadn't been enough to save him. The judge donned the black cap and sentenced him to be hanged until dead in Aberdeen on 17th May. But thanks to a surge of public sympathy across the city and the county, that was not the end of the story. Thousands of signatures poured in pleading for a reprieve for Stephen, and the jury wrote a letter setting out why they had felt unable to recommend the man to mercy at the trial. An application was made for an examination of the condemned man under the Lunacy Act. In the end Stephen was reprieved and lived out the rest of his years in a ward for lunatics, as people with mental health difficulties were then known.

A Case of Amnesia?

This episode from April 1864 remains one of the most notorious canal crimes ever committed and at the time at the time it stirred a widespread sensation. Among the readers poring over the contemporary newspaper reports was Robert Louis Stevenson, then an imaginative 14-year-old who had been born only ten miles from the site of the drama. The case may have helped to cultivate his early fascination with character, and the inner battle to suppress evil instincts that might be lurking within the individual. These were among the themes he would explore later in his *Strange Case of Dr Jekyll and Mr Hyde*, which was published in 1886. Readers can judge for themselves how far the novel chimes with events that unfolded on the banks of the Union Canal.

Thirty-year-old carter George Bryce lived at the inn at Ratho. On a Saturday morning in April he rose at about six o'clock, hung around the yard and an hour later went out, leaving behind his horse and cart. He crossed the canal bridge and walked towards the villa belonging to the merchant Robert Todd. Near the gate he passed a boy carrying a tray with the morning's loaves and greeted him chirpily with the Scots term for a baker's man: "Fine mornin', Batchie!" Todd was away on business, as he often was—he owned a mill at Leith, among other concerns. Also living at the villa were his wife and 11-year-old daughter who were both called Margaret. They were served by the 23-year-old nursemaid from North Queensferry named Jeannie Seaton, and a cook called Isabella Brown. Bryce had some time ago fallen in love with Isabella, and they had begun to spend time together.

The Bryces were a family of fourteen siblings, many of whom had married and moved out. Some of the brothers had joined their father John in running the inn and working for his other business as a coal and stone merchant. George had always struck his father as different from the others. He would stare into space, mutter to himself or wander off. He had made so little progress at school that his father encouraged him to leave early and set him to work driving carts, often to the station or the nearby quarry. Across the canal, the neighbour Mrs Todd was undecided as to whether George was shy by nature, or just plain sulky.

George was in the habit of rattling into Gogar Station in flamboyant style. He would greet station master James Meikle with a military salute, saying: "How are ye today, Colonel?" Or he would tug the man's whiskers and enquire after his wife, though he knew perfectly well that Meikle had no wife. If George found some amusement in these eccentric familiarities, the station master took a dim view.

Often, Meikle would ask an acquaintance who happened to be in the station to assist him with a small task, but he would never ask the Ratho carter. He'd sooner trust a ten-year-old, he said, than half-daft George Bryce.

In the 1850s, George had joined the militia and been away at camp for a year and a half. Military life brought about a change in him, and not for the better. This deterioration may well have resulted from brutal treatment. Though there were calls to end the physical punishment of military men, those who were found wanting—who reported for duty drunk or were inattentive, for example—could be flogged till the skin hung off their backs. George was a well-built man, but his temperament would have made him a vulnerable figure in the military camp. Moreover, as his family had noted, he couldn't hold his liquor. His brother-in-law William Wilson, a porter at Ratho station, observed that George could turn violent when drunk.

After five years of military life George resumed carting, though all was not well with him. He would go missing for days, abandoning his horse and cart in the road. He drank heavily and was troubled with insomnia, which left him exhausted. George began to take his Sunday meal in the furthest corner of the parlour, away from the family. In the village, unscrupulous locals would steer him to the pub and lean on him to buy rounds of drink. A favourite escapist haunt of his was the woods on Lord Morton's estate. During a ramble there in 1857 he bumped into two footmen and a gamekeeper. After a brief jokey exchange, a gamekeeper gently tapped the carter on the shoulder, correcting something he had said. Bryce's face changed dramatically, taking on a wild look. He drew a clasp-knife and threatened to stab anyone who challenged him. The gamekeepers called the constable, James Wright, who persuaded him to hand over the knife and accompanied him home. Once George was in bed the constable recommended his father to keep a careful eye on him. Bryce later claimed to have no recollection of this incident—though the constable took this with a pinch of salt.

George's thoughts turned to suicide. He once told one of his sisters: "I'll soon be in eternity," and was found half an hour later in the stable with a rope round his neck, the other end tied to a beam. On another occasion, George was found after a two-day absence buried beneath the straw, with a knife at his side. He'd intended to cut his throat, he said. As the family's concerns grew, his brother William was persuaded to sleep beside him with one eye open.

Matters got worse. On the 10th of March the carter began drinking heavily in the presence of Isabella. This brought any affection she may have had for him to an abrupt end. When she resolved not to see him again, George grew angry. He formed the view that one person was to blame for the cook's coolness—the nursemaid, Jeannie Seaton. He believed Seaton had long held a low opinion of him and had poisoned Isabella's mind against him by calling him a "drunken blackguard." For two nights in a row he did not sleep at the inn, but hid among the straw. On Friday morning he resumed work carting, came home and went to bed early. On the Saturday he woke an hour after William. That was when he milled about in the yard before he setting off across the canal bridge, having said he was off to the station. After hailing the baker's boy he leapt the wall of Todd's villa to find Isabella at the back door. He angrily demanded she tell him the whereabouts of Jeannie.

Getting no answer, he burst in the back door and made for the nursery. There he grabbed Seaton, threw her down and began to assault her. Margaret Todd bravely grabbed an umbrella and began to beat him with it. As she did so she was struck by the brutal and detached look on his face, as though he barely recognised his victim. Mrs Todd's onslaught forced him to let Seaton go and she shouted at the nursemaid to make a run for it. Todd then seized the carter by the wrists, but he escaped her grip and started after his quarry. Seaton leapt the villa wall and tore away as far as am unused old building known as the Old Distillery. There Bryce caught up with her there and threw her down, pinning his knee to her shoulder. By the time a few local men arrived to help, she was in a sorry state. Bryce had taken a razor to her throat and scored a deep gash on one side. Locals managed to pull him off and Seaton was carried into a neighbour's house and laid on a mattress, where she lay bleeding profusely. She managed to whisper that she wanted water. Meanwhile, a constable and a quarry worker went after the killer. He threatened that he would take his own life or use the razor on them before they caught him. Ten minutes after her request for water, Jeannie Seaton was dead.

Bryce was taken to Calton Jail in Edinburgh where he was visited by two medics. Dr Robert Ritchie visited three times to question him about the murder and explore his history. When Bryce said he could not recall seeing Seaton or assaulting her, the medic believed him. Ritchie took the view that the earlier incident in Lord Morton's Woods indicated an impulsive tendency that had worsened to the point of insanity. The next expert to examine him, Professor Haycock, saw him on two occasions. Haycock's quaint observations owe something to phrenology, the study of discerning a person's character from bumps on the skull, which was controversial even then. He observed that Bryce had a small head and receding forehead, which was "often the case among persons of low organization". He also declared the carter insane. At the time of the attack, said the professor, he was suffering from a form of maniacal excitement.

In court, Bryce pled not guilty. Although he recalled going to Mr Todd's house that morning he strongly maintained he had no recollection of seeing Seaton. He also believed she had called him a drunken blackguard, though she had denied this. The proof of insanity, it was argued, lay in the fact that he could not remember having done the deed. After only 45 minutes the jury returned a verdict of guilty, recommending mercy on account of Bryce's low mental organization. Accounts of the frenzied nature of the crime, reports on the trial proceedings and speculation as to Bryce's mental state boosted newspaper sales. Before a vast crowd of onlookers, Bryce was hanged at the traditional spot at the head of Libberton's Wynd in Edinburgh, like William Burke and scores of others before him. He would become infamous not only for the ferocity of the murder, but also for being the last person to be hanged in public in the capital. The story went that the executioner, James Askern, had used a short drop that left Bryce to struggle for some time, stirring restlessness among the crowd. However, "botched" executions were not particularly unusual.

The two medical experts believed that their interviews had revealed a man insane and incapable of recollecting his violent act. But it is possible that Bryce was smarter than he appeared and had misled them in attempt to save his skin. On the day of the murder, when apprehended by the constable and the quarryman, it was put to him that he had cut a woman's neck. He replied: "She's cheap of what she's got." This suggested that at the time he had full knowledge of what he had done. In the days before the execution, rumours began to spread that Bryce's profession of amnesia had been a lie concocted to fool the medics and save his skin. The Todd family later marked their loss by erecting a stone in memory of the nursemaid.

The Upturned Chair

In the 1870s, James Munn, his wife Mary and their five children were living in Glasgow. Thirty-four-year-old James was often away from home working as a steward aboard two of the popular tourist paddle steamers, the Iona and the Islay, which plied the Crinan Canal between Glasgow and the Western Isles. At the end of the decade the family uprooted to Argyll and by the time of the incident in 1882 were running a canalside inn at lock 5, two and a half miles from Lochgilphead. The small, close-knit settlement of Cairnbaan had sprung up in the early 1800s with the coming of the waterway. The Munns provided sailors, merchants and other travellers with food and accommodation in a setting that was beautiful but, thanks to a tempestuous family life, not necessarily peaceful.

Twenty-four-year-old Mary Rowan served at the inn and lived with her parents on the opposite bank. At supper with the Munns on 13th January, Rowan noticed that six-months-pregnant Mrs Munn was slightly tipsy, which was not unknown, though her husband was sober. At about seven the Munns set out for an evening in Lochgilphead, leaving Rowan to look after the children and put them to bed. Rowan returned to her own house later, after the Munn's return—but her sleep would be too brief. At 5 o'clock in the morning, she was wakened by a pounding at the door. It was James Munn, saying that his wife had taken gravely ill, and asking Rowan to come back to the inn. He suspected a miscarriage.

Rowan got up and followed Munn across the canal bridge. She climbed the stairs to the room where Mrs Munn lay. What she found was a harrowing scene. Blood was everywhere. Mrs Munn lay in bed, clad only in a chemise and half-wrapped in bedclothes soaked with blood: it had seeped across the floor and under the table, except for a single patch where James Munn had apparently tried to clean up. Incapable of speaking, Mrs Munn let forth a series of groans. Two of the children played in their bed in the room, strangely oblivious. Mary Rowan took a petticoat to wipe some of the stains off the floor and placed this in a basin of water, which quickly blushed pink. She then left the inn and went to ask for help from her mother, Sarah.

When Sarah Rowan arrived she stepped around an empty bottle of porter and a chair that had been left upturned by the bed. She felt the woman's feet and found them cold despite the blazing fire. She then lifted the covers to find no sign of miscarriage. Munn asked the mother and daughter, "Can I give her anything?" They shook their heads. They doubted if anything could be done. James Munn circled the bed, crying and caressing his wife ineffectually, with her condition all the while worsening. Another neighbour, Malcolm McKellar, was summoned, who asked Munn what had happened. Munn replied that he didn't know. He believed his wife blamed him for her condition, but he denied it and speculated that the upturned chair might something to do with it. Perhaps she had tried to stand on it and lost her footing. McKellar asked if she had been drinking. Munn admitted the bottle of porter had been full the night before, so she had taken a little, but not too much. McKellar said they must get medical help and set off in a dog-cart for Lochgilphead.

By the time two medics arrived at nine in the morning, Mrs Munn had died. It was later said that Mrs Munn might have lived, had a doctor been called straight away. Drs Macnaughton and Hunter were closely followed by two policemen, Constable William Munro and the Argyll chief constable, Colin Mackay. Dr Hunter drew Mackay's attention to a deep cut on the body and declared that they need look no further for the cause of death. The police then began a search. There was no weapon in the room but downstairs they recovered four breakfast knives, all without stain of blood, though a fifth could not be accounted for. Following a post-mortem the doctors compiled a report that made for chilling reading. There had been no miscarriage. The woman's body bore twenty-two bruises, some of them very recent, to the ribs, legs, arms, shoulders and jawbone, the latter having the appearance of thumb marks. The fatal injury was a wound nearly two inches long and two inches deep. It went upwards into the body, though strangely another wound entered through the same opening at a right angle. The doctors concluded this could not have been inflicted by a fall from a chair, as James Munn had claimed. They were sure it had been caused by a knife. Few in the village would have been surprised. James Munn had been known to kick and punch his wife on a regular basis. All three inn servants—Rowan, Flora MacPherson and Ann Maclevin—had seen him striking her.

From the turn of the year, events were hurtling towards their dreadful conclusion. On New Year's Day, Mrs Munn had arrived at the Rowans' house sporting a black eye. Though she never actually blamed her husband, it was clear that she sought refuge from him, and it only after considerable persuasion from him that she agreed to return home. Enmeshed in these clashes was frequent drinking and mutual claims of unfaithfulness. Mary Munn accused her spouse of carrying on with the maids and her father, Peter McCulloch, had seen Munn driving another woman in his cart. The overwhelmed Mary Munn had attempted to take her life by throwing herself into the canal. John Black, the lock-keeper, saw her stumble into the canal in the October before her death, though she later emerged dripping from head to foot. A few weeks later Munn warned Black that wife was threatening to throw herself into the canal; he was unable to keep her in. In the week before her death, Mrs Munn had disturbed Macpherson and MacLevin in the night by wandering in a drunken state, slamming doors. Goings-on such as screaming and drunken quarrelling had become so troublesome that that a farm servant who lodged at the inn, Donald Dewar, felt obliged to move out. Only three days before her death, Mary Munn confided in MacPherson that her husband was denying paternity of her baby. She was in terror of him taking her life after finding a knife under his pillow. She confided in a local woman, Anne MacLevin, that she lived in terror of her husband taking her life.

The innkeeper's protestations of innocence were to no avail. Despite his story that his wife had died by falling onto an upturned chair, he was arrested and detained at Inveraray Jail on a charge of striking his wife and murdering her by stabbing in the abdomen with a knife. The trial at the High Court in Edinburgh began in March, with Munn pleading not guilty. Much evidence was given as to the state of the Munns' marriage. John Simpson, a local writer to the signet who had dealings with the couple since they moved to the area said that for the past year they had led a 'cat and dog sort of life'. Dr Hunter reiterated that he had never seen a wound of this kind caused by a blunt instrument such as the leg of chair. Even supposing one cut had been made by the leg of the chair, he could not say how it could have also caused the other cut. Dr Macnaughton concurred.

Mrs Munn's character did not emerge untarnished. Macpherson had left service at the inn because of Mrs Munn's having scolded her; and a year before her death another female servant had been assaulted by her. This had triggered her first attempt to drown herself in the canal and seems to have marked the chaotic turn in the family's lifestyle. Her father, Peter McCulloch, who was harbourmaster of Ardrishaig, reluctantly admitted to the court that he had seen his daughter under the influence of drink and had on occasions had to keep her down and put her to bed. She had spat on him, used coarse language and argued with her mother. With so much emphasis on domestic disharmony and violence, the evidence was stacking heavily against James Munn.

Yet the trial was about to take an unexpected turn with the testimony of Dr Joseph Bell, the expert witness who would later be famed as the inspiration for Sherlock Holmes. A tutor at Edinburgh's medical school, Bell was known for the shrewd insights he gleaned by closely observing his patients' clothing and characteristics, an ability that was much admired by former medical student and later author Arthur Conan Doyle. Bell's evidence was strongly reminiscent of the fictional detective's deductive methods, not least in the dramatic flourish he offered as a conclusion. Bell told the court he had made a special study of cases like Mrs Munn's. In at least eight instances injuries of this kind had not been caused by a sharp instrument. He didn't know how the second cut to Mrs Munn could have been made by a knife, because the slightest change in its direction would have produced a ragged edge. He was suggesting that a sharp kick from behind had resulted in Mrs Munn being impaled on the leg of an upturned chair. This unorthodox view was also put forward by Dr Alexander Keillner, who said injuries of this kind were rare, and the wound was caused by pressure on the sharp edge of a bone.

In his summing up the Lord Justice Clerk noted that this was a case of conflicting evidence. The Munns had enjoyed an amicable evening out, but James Munn was not without malice towards his wife and there was no doubt they had led a very unhappy life. He described the evidence put forward by the Edinburgh doctors as 'of a very remarkable character', perhaps hinting that he believed it to be fanciful; and Dr Hunter, he said, had had the best opportunity to examine the wounds after the incident. It was the jury's task to decide whether they were satisfied that the wounds had been caused by a knife. Perhaps there was great reluctance to settle on a verdict that would see James Munn hanged. It took the jury only eight minutes to find him not guilty of murdering his wife with a knife. It seems that the innkeeper had a cohort of local supporters for the announcement was received with applause, which the judge hastily supressed.

Before long, the inn had become a much more peaceful place. It was as though the new owner, James Fraser, wished to signal to the public that he was drawing a line under those unthinkable past events. He turned the establishment into a temperance retreat. In the mid-1890s, he invited prospective patrons to while away their stay at Cairnbaan in trout fishing in the hill lochs or the sea.

The Standalane Case

Throughout the nineteenth and early twentieth century, the discovery of a body in Scotland's lowland canals was a regular occurrence. Amid the dismal economic circumstances of the late 1930s, the number of instances reported in the press rose steeply, the Dalmuir vicinity of the Forth and Clyde amassing a particularly high body count. Local casualties that decade included cleansing department employee John Tait, plumber John Irwin, tram driver William Sawyers, labourer Charles Lees and, separately, two women named as Jean Young and a Mrs Bell. In such cases death by drowning was presumed, though no one could be sure whether it had been by accident or design. In the case of Young, it was hinted that suicide was possible since she had long been in poor health. However, another female death on a wild night in December 1938 had sinister overtones.

Retired engine driver William Brown tended his allotment at Dalmuir on the south bank. It had just gone ten when he heard a desperate shout go up. Brown was in no doubt that someone needed help. He left his garden plot and dashed towards the source of the cry. Close to the farmhouse of Standalane Cottage he came across a grey-haired man standing shivering on the path, his trousers soaked through. "My wife's in the water," said the man. "What will ye do? I'm all wet." He added that his wife had been at his side when she jumped away without warning, though what happened after that he hadn't been able to see. Brown ran off to get a boat hook. By the time he got back, strangely, the man had disappeared. He let the hook out on the canal and began to cast about till he'd got a hold of something. He turned the pole and pulled towards the bank. He saw with a chill that it was the lifeless body of a woman. A passer-by, Mark McElhinney, helped him to bring the body ashore, and Brown raised the alarm at the local police office.

At the scene shortly afterwards were Sergeant Alexander MacLean and Detective Inspector George Stalker. MacLean's attempt at artificial respiration was to no avail. Stalker noted a number of scratches to the woman's face, though there was no sign of a struggle having taken place. The mystery man having reappeared, he was taken to the police station to give his version of events. He was Charles Conway Hunter, a 57-year-old gardener who picked up jobs here and there. He lived at Second Avenue, Clydebank, with his now-deceased wife, Edith and their three daughters. The couple had usually ventured out on Friday evenings. They were walking on the towpath arm-in-arm, he said, when Edith asked if she could swap to the canal side to avoid potholes. Moments later he heard a splash. "I tried to save her, but it was hopeless," he said.

Stalker had a policeman's instinct. On arrival at the scene he had entertained suspicions, and on top of that the sole witness account struck him as unconvincing. Looking over Hunter's hands for signs of a struggle, he saw that the nails on the right hand were cut to the quick, while those on the left were an eighth of an inch longer. His colleagues agreed this was odd, but stronger evidence would be needed to justify detaining him. The gardener was freed at 6 o'clock on the Saturday evening. Stalker spoke to police casualty surgeon George McKendrick following an examination of the injuries to the woman's neck. McKendrick concurred that this could be a case of murder. In the following days Stalker returned to the scene, again seeking signs of a struggle but finding nothing. He also carried out a home-made experiment. He fashioned a dummy in the shape of a human figure and filled it with sand until it weighed ten stone, approximately the weight of the woman. He let it float on the canal and observed the way it floated from the bank. Though he would readily admit this was not robustly scientific, it served to convince him further.

A post-mortem was conducted by John Glaister, professor of forensic science at Glasgow University, assisted by a Dr Price. Glaister was internationally renowned for his expertise and was often the first port-of-call where an act of violence was suspected. He concluded that Edith had died of cardiac arrest, triggered by asphyxia, and with no conclusive signs of drowning. The following weekend Hunter was arrested and charged with having murdered his wife by striking her on the face and forehead, compressing her throat and throttling her. When cautioned he continued to maintain his innocence, saying: "I never did anything like that. I never put a hand on the woman."

The High Court trial on 28th February did not lack drama, with a further family tragedy occurring elsewhere on the first day. Conway Hunter entered a plea of not guilty. A story of family adversity began to emerge. Two of the couple's daughters, Elsie Hunter and Alice Kent, were called as witnesses. The Hunters had been unable to afford a home of their own and lodged in the room of a house owned by a woman called Elizabeth Hendry. Edith worried about her daughter, Mary Preston, who had been ill for some time and had two young children to look after. Twenty-three-year-old Elsie had only recently got out of the sanatorium. Worse still, the family mourned the loss of a son who had died three years before. Edith had been a sensitive, highly-strung type at the best of times, and the bereavement had led to periods of depression. Also, Edith's health was less sound. About three weeks before her death, she had called the landlady to her room, complaining of a pain in her heart, and had fearfully gripped her tightly by the hand, but after about a quarter of an hour the pain went away. Kent confirmed that her mother used to complain of pain around the heart. However, no one noticed any sign of thoughts of suicide and Kent rejected any suggestion that it had been an unhappy marriage. Her parents got on well and her father was an even-tempered man. They had indeed gone out every Friday evening together and none of the sisters had ever seen any violence between them. This impression was borne out by Elizabeth Hendry. The day's proceedings over, the Hunter sisters left court to be given some bad news. Their ailing sister Mary had passed away.

The trial resumed with evidence from Inspector Stalker, and almost a full day was given to testimonies from the medical experts. Professor Glaister described the injuries to the neck that he believed resulted from grasping by a hand or hands with considerable force. Having examined tissue from the bruised areas under the microscope he concluded that they had been produced while she was still alive. Edith Hunter was dead when her body entered the water, he thought. In response to questions from the judge, Lord Aitchison, Glaister stated that he believed her death could not have been by accident or suicide. In his view she had been throttled, leading to a fatal heart attack. He did not think that her heart condition alone was the cause. Glaister's assistant, Dr Price added that the throttling must have continued for at least half a minute. A Dr Henderson had made an x-ray examination on November 22nd of the hyoid bone from the neck of Mrs Hunter, the bone just slightly below the Adam's apple, and found a fracture which he thought occurred before death. This was confirmed by Professor Sydney Smith, of Edinburgh University, who had carefully considered the post-mortem reports and found nothing to indicate death from drowning. He echoed the view that it was caused by manual strangulation, probably by severe pressure. The only departure from this wealth of medical evidence was offered by Dr Alexander Lyall, assistant Royal Infirmary surgeon, appearing for the defence. He postulated that the fracture to the hyoid bone could have been caused by coming into contact with the boatman's hook used by Brown to take the body from the water.

The charge was reduced to manslaughter and the jury of ten women and five men found the accused guilty. Passing sentence, Lord Aitchison said that he had difficulty in pronouncing a proper sentence as he did not really know what had happened. The ordeal of the loss of their mother and sister, and now the conviction of their father following unpleasant medical evidence, was too much for the two surviving Hunter sisters. As their father was sentenced to five years' penal servitude they wept openly in the court.

CHAPTER FIVE : A HIGHLANDER ABROAD

Doing a Muirachan

For decades Highlanders had made the long journey to the Lowlands for trade, not least when they drove cattle south for sale at Falkirk. The opening of the northern canals—the Crinan in 1801 and the Caledonian in 1822—created fresh economic opportunities for northerners wishing to migrate temporarily. They could labour in the rich agricultural fields of the Lothians, earn a wage at manufactories such as the dye works in Glasgow, or sell home-grown produce. When Alexander McKinnon arrived in Glasgow from Tiree in May 1828, he had a large batch of eggs to sell. He had come from the sunniest and most westerly isle of the Inner Hebrides by boat. Whether any of his eggs were scrambled by the choppy seas is not known, but on arrival he had enough of them intact to allow him to make a handsome profit. The night was still young by the time he had sold the lot. He set off for a night out carrying £10. This was a handsome sum, far more than the amount a labourer could earn in a few months, but he would later stick to the story that this was the profit from the eggs.

Lacking a proper money purse, he tucked it into his stockings: £2 in silver and some coppers in one leg and £8 in notes in the other. The Glasgow magistrates had stepped up security in recent years in attempt to deter an increasing vagrant population and fearful of the potential threat to public order as migrants from Ireland and Highlands converged on the city and competed to make a living. MacKinnon would have passed several of the watchmen who were on duty that night. At that time, approximately 102 night watches were concentrated within the Royalty of the city, north of the River Clyde, each beat numbered and mapped out. The watchman was to look for signs of anything unusual on his patch, ready to intervene in the event of trouble, and he was required to take note of any idle or suspicious-looking person loitering or passing through the area. It would have been difficult for anyone to commit a crime without being seen.

The Tiree man was alone in a strange metropolis and couldn't speak a word of English, but that didn't put him off the idea of a good night on the town. In the city's Maxwell Street things he was pleased to meet a young Irishwoman who readily befriended him. Isabella McMenemy, known to her friends as Bell, was short in stature with a fresh, pale complexion and reddish hair. She was attractive, and had draped about her shoulders a grey mantle lined with red silk. She had arrived from County Tyrone in 1821, and it was possible that she comprehended a little of the Highlander's speech thanks to Irish Gaelic. A handloom worker, she appeared intelligent and made for engaging company. The couple warmed themselves over a gill or two of whisky and Bell invited MacKinnon to a house on the south side of the city. They crossed the Broomielaw Bridge over the River Clyde and headed towards the aqueduct at Port Eglinton, the basin of the Glasgow, Paisley and Ardrossan Canal. En route they met a watchman, who exchanged a few words with McMenemy.

Travellers had been drawn increasingly to the Paisley Canal by faster boats, but by the time McMenemy and McKinnon arrived no one was likely to be milling about: the final passenger vessel had left in the late afternoon. The couple passed the bustle of the basin, with its night cargo boats and, leaving behind the lights of the canal inn, they went westwards along the towpath into the darkness. Under an aqueduct bridge, McMenemy slowed her pace. She invited MacKinnon to stop and sit down, but he refused. Perhaps a sixth sense was telling him something unpleasant might be afoot. Beneath the aqueduct they were joined by a man McMenemy introduced as her brother, and then a second man stepped out of the darkness. McKinnon felt himself grabbed by the neck cloth, and twisted until he was on the point of choking. The struggle went on and McMenemy stepped in, showing her true colours. She seized a brick and struck MacKinnon several blows to the head, sending him to the ground, out cold.

By the time McKinnon came round the gang of assailants had fled. His shoes had gone missing along with one stocking and all the silver and coppers he'd been hiding in it. Though he was badly injured, McKinnon managed to raise himself up from the pool of blood he was lying in and found his stocking, but not his shoes nor the money. He set off in search of help. He found watchman William Brown of the Gorbals Police Office and led him to the site of the attack. At two o'clock in the morning, when McKinnon was being treated for his injuries, Brown returned with colleague Thomas Laurieston. They caught sight of two men at the aqueduct bridge who were scraping the ground as if trying to cover the blood. The men claimed they were from Paisley and were just looking at the blood. After this they ran off.

Soon afterwards Laurieston caught sight of Bell McMenemy and tried to get a hold of her. She escaped his grip by wriggling free of her mantle. When the watchman lifted it off the ground, he saw that it was covered in blood. He pursued McMenemy to a house, the lodging house of a couple named McQueen. Mrs McQueen, not understanding what was going on, shut the door in the officer's face. Laurieston picked up a shoe McMenemy had dropped and went to get Brown. The pair were admitted to the house and made a search. A man was lying on the bed, who turned out to be a well-known ne'er-do-well of Irish extraction named Thomas Connor. They continued their search for McMenemy and found her cowering in a chest. She angrily through the ill-gotten gains on the bed. Connor protested that he had had nothing to do with the affair, and McMenemy had stolen the money acting alone.

By that September, the police had rounded up a gang of four suspects. A gang of four appeared before the Glasgow circuit court charged with the assault and robbery on the Highlander on the banks of the Paisley Canal. They were Charles Hill, Hugh Richardson, Thomas Connor and Bell McMenemy. McKinnon, who had suffered lasting harm from the attack, gave his evidence through an interpreter. He identified Richardson as the person who seized him by the neck cloth. Richardson and Hill pleaded not guilty while the other two initially pleaded guilty. At the trial, the evidence of the watchmen did much to establish the movements of the two principals. Background as to goings-on at the lodging house was filled in by Robert McQueen. McMenemy had left the house at quarter to nine on the evening in question. She returned about 3 o'clock in the morning, asking be let in and saying she could be murdered if the landlord didn't admit her. Connor followed soon after. The pair asked McQueen if he would go out into the street to retrieve the missing mantle for them but he refused to get involved.

After Connor had gone to bed that McQueen noticed the bloodstains on his shirt and vest and the following morning Connor replied that he had been "doing a Muirachan". The *Perthshire Courier*, reporting on the case, explained to its genteel readers that the word "Muirachan" meant a Highlandman. Conner's ready use of this phrase suggests that roughing up a visitor from the north was a sport familiar to him, as a fully paid-up member of the criminal classes. Connor changed into a jacket and trousers and asked McQueen if he could leave to go to the canal in search of money but he refused. Connor's main regret, which he aired to McQueen, was that in the course of the assault they had taken off the wrong stocking: they understood that there were eight pounds in the other stocking. He also admitted to McQueen that the robbery had been planned and that he had been lying in wait under the aqueduct bridge to attack McKinnon. Connor later changed his plea to not guilty; but this did little to improve his situation. Lord Meadowbank had met him in court before. Six years previously he been charged with stealing a £20 note and twenty-three shillings from a man in Bridgeton. He had only got off with this because the jury found the case not proven. He was a well-known criminal, said Lord Meadowbank, who should have taken heed of his previous close call. Connor should entertain no hope of mercy since the crime could have resulted in the death of McKinnon. However, McMenemy was the more guilty of the two, and there was no escaping it was a capital crime.

Richardson and Hill were found not guilty. Connor was pronounced guilty but recommended to mercy by the jury on account of that he was only 22 years of age. McMenemy, not much older, was found guilty in terms of her own confession. Both prisoners burst into tears and Connor begged to be spared his life. His Lordship implored them to make their peace with an offended God and sentenced them to be hanged in front of the jail on Wednesday twenty-third October. It was seldom, remarked Lord Meadowbank, that the full sentence of the law was brought to bear on females. Connor sarcastically thanked his Lordship for the justice he had done them and went on to accuse a witness of having sworn falsely against him. McMenemy was about to add to his performance when the pair of them were silenced by hurrying them away from the bar.

On the evening preceding the execution McMenemy sobbed and fervently confessed her sins to the Catholic clergymen who attended her until 10 o'clock. At 8 o'clock the next morning the condemned pair were dressed in black and taken from their cells. The crowd was larger than usual, with the most exaggerated figure suggesting 50,000 spectators. McMenemy's execution attracted a great deal of attention as she was believed to be the first woman executed in Glasgow for 32 years. The crowd rippled with gossip of the pair's colourful history and their modus operandi as partners-in-crime. It was known that McMenemy had been employed at a factory and got to know Connor through a female friend. She was cast as the femme fatale who would decoy men, usually the worse for drink, onto roads and paths on the outskirts of the city, where Connor would knock the victim down and steal his possessions. Connor, also born in County Tyrone, was described as a bad sort ever since he had been able to crawl, who had never followed any sort of occupation. He had been in trouble with the law several times. He was reckoned to have had an unfortunate upbringing and a mother who egged him on in his crimes.

The caps were drawn over their faces and prayers continued until Connor gave the hangman his signal by dropping a handkerchief. It was later said that the executioner did not give McMenemy enough rope, for she was visible by the crowd down to her feet and was seen to be struggling. After the usual period of hanging the bodies were taken down. Though McMenemy and Connor's careers might be at an end, an opportunist of a different criminal hue was waiting in the wings. Immediately after the hanging, a man with the appearance of a labourer appeared. He demanded the bodies, saying he that by prior arrangement he had a cart waiting to convey the couple's bodies to a house where their friends lived. Fortunately, it was realised that he was not genuine. When challenged, the aspiring resurrectionist made a run for it and disappeared.

At the time of the attack on MacKinnon northern migrants to the Lowlands were depicted in stereotypical ways. The Highlander was seen as the rustic whose lack of nous was likely to be exploited by the more sophisticated lowland inhabitant. The traveller's vulnerability could be apparent as soon as he or she disembarked from a boat: cautionary tales circulated of shore porters creating a distraction by offering to help with luggage, while an accomplice skilfully rifled in a pocket. Nervousness of travel to and from the Lowlands was reflected in Gaelic verse warning of ruthless city folk seeking to exploit the visitor's relative naivety. Mutual prejudices aside, the migrants were right to be wary. MacKinnon had been attacked for the same reasons as many a victim of theft is attacked: he was alone in a strange, foreign-speaking environment and his assailants knew he was carrying money. The gang of four had carefully planned for Bell to lure him along the canal to the aqueduct. It was not the first time such a setting had been chosen as the stage for an unpleasant assault, and it would not be the last.

A Forlorn Hope

One Saturday at the end of October 1821, the steam boat Highlander was getting ready to leave Fort William. A tall, thin man wrapped in a tartan cloak got aboard. He was using a steamboat passenger service that had been running for only a few months between there and Glasgow. Highlander had the paddle-power to negotiate the rugged coast and wild currents of the West Coast with relative ease, yet boasted slim proportions that could fit through the locks of the Crinan Canal, making for a journey that was celebrated as the last word in safety, comfort and speed. The steamboats were primarily for tourists from the Lowlands and further afield, with stops at islands such as Iona and Staffa varying to suit the particular the sightseeing wish lists of the passengers. Though advertised as affordable, the fare of £2 or more and a separate bill for breakfast and dinner was probably beyond reach for the many island inhabitants who had to live at subsistence level, and many had been a little wary of the effect the new-fangled steamboats might have on their world from their inception in 1820.

The man in the tartan cloak would not have been conspicuous. Such boats usually featured a bagpiper swathed in tartan to pipe the passengers aboard, announce mealtimes and play a bedtime serenade—whether the passengers wanted it or not. The passenger list would have been nothing if not varied, likely including tourists from south of the border, mainland Scots, Hebrideans, and respectable folk rubbing shoulders with the lower orders. The tall man wore blue trousers and his whiskers straggled over his young-looking features so that his face couldn't easily be made out. The folds of his cloak had been carefully arranged so that nobody notice the one feature that would mark him out from the crowd—his left arm was missing from the elbow. The tall man stayed aboard for the whole four-day journey, which would entail stops on demand and to take on board a fresh supply of coals. There would be a brief night-time stay onshore at Crinan at the westernmost extremity of the canal. Then, at first light the passengers would re-embark to pass through the fifteen locks, a tedious process that could take six hours or more. Having negotiated that, the passengers would make a final overnight stop in Lochgilphead, where they would be lucky to secure one of the village's limited number of beds before resuming for the last day's travel to Glasgow.

At the Broomielaw, amid a swirl of bodies, coal smoke and luggage, the tall man disembarked with the other passengers and was seen a short time later in the city's Jamaica Street. He proceeded from there Moodie's Court, an undistinguished lane of offices, stables and taverns, where he took a room in the lodging house of Catherine McDonald. On the Tuesday morning the traveller got up early and, dressed in a suit of black clothing, he settled his account with Mrs MacDonald and began walking the short distance to Maxwell Street. He was certainly going up in the world. He arrived at the Eagle

Inn, haunt of the rich and noble, where he announced himself to as Admiral Sir Thomas Maitland. The Admiral straight away made the innkeeper, Daniel McDonald, aware of his needs and wants. He wished to have the attention of a personal hairdresser, said he, since his appearance had become a little dishevelled following a long journey on the Highlander steamboat. He also required a chaise to be brought, as he would later be going out on business. Within minutes, Admiral Maitland was in a luxurious room upstairs being attended to by a Mr Ritchie, the barber. Once the naval officer was expressing satisfaction with his now highly-powdered appearance, he put on a new-looking hat and tilted it down over his eyes. These sartorial adjustments made, the Admiral took himself downstairs and clambered aboard the waiting chaise. He instructed the driver, Richard Spencer, to make for the Royal Bank in Queen Street and wait for him outside.

Inside the Royal Bank, teller John Thompson was working in a room of his own. The door opened and here was an unfamiliar customer whose appearance Thomson found odd. He looked like his head had been thrust into a bag of flour and he held his hat in a forced-looking manner over his left arm. The customer handed over a note authorising the payment of £90 sterling from the account of Sir Thomas Maitland KCB, Admiral of the Royal Navy, this sum to be debited from his account with Smith, Payne and Smiths, Bankers, of Mansion House, London. Thompson was uneasy about handing over the money. The wording of the note was unusual and there was an unexpected spelling mistake. Moreover, the person before him did not have the bearing of a high-ranking military man, and might even be insane. Thompson came to a decision. He told the customer that, though it was an awkward thing to refuse a nobleman of his rank, he couldn't give him the cash because he didn't know him, so the Admiral should go to another bank. The customer replied testily that any bank would willingly discount the bill. With this he strode back to the chaise, ordering Spencer to hurry him back to the Eagle Inn. He was soon upstairs taking a restorative glass of brandy and calling for a pen and paper.

The Admiral wasn't finished with his driver yet. In a short time they were back on the road, bound this time for the Thistle Bank in Virginia Street. With his left hand apparently tucked firmly into his pocket, he used his right to push the draft, somewhat clumsily, towards the teller, Robert McNair. McNair looked over the draft for 90 pounds and enquired whether he was the person named on the bill, or merely his representative. The man replied that he was Admiral Maitland of the Royal Navy, but McNair doubted this as the man's bearing did not match his social station. He concluded that the man before him must be Maitland's servant and sent him on his way, saying it would not be convenient to discount the bill.

McNair at the Thistle had given him the second rebuff of the morning, but the Admiral was not for giving up. Within minutes he set Spencer driving to 642 Argyle Street, at the foot of Glassford Street. Here was the home of the Ship Bank, otherwise known as Carrick's Bank, and perhaps the timing of the Admiral's visit here would turn out to be propitious. For many years the Ship had been managed attentively by one Robin Carrick, who was among Glasgow's wealthiest men. Like many a great man of business, Carrick was as admired for his success as he was despised for his miserliness. It so happened that the well-known penny-raker had died a few months previously, and hopes were stirring that a more lax regime might now prevail at the bank, a situation that could work in a customer's favour. On the other hand, cracks were beginning to appear in the Admiral's presentation. Amid the grime and bustle of the city streets, the powder on his head had begun to wash away, his whiskers began to look bedraggled and his clothing had become unkempt. Stepping down from the chaise he neglected to conceal the missing left arm, which drew the attention of a porter stationed nearby.

Inside the Ship, the Admiral visibly attempted to compose himself and presented the draft to Michael Rowand, cashier and partner. Rowand was immediately suspicious. He wouldn't hand out any money unless the customer could prove his identity. The Admiral said he was known to a minister in the Gorbals. He went away and returned a few minutes later with the signature of the Reverend Dr James

McLean appended to the bank draft. At the sight of the clergyman's signature, Rowand relented and paid out the amount. Shortly before four o'clock the Admiral emerged from the Ship with a large wad of notes and instructed Spencer to take him back to the Eagle Inn. On arrival, Maitland waved the driver away, handing him a note and went inside to order dinner for two. By early evening Michael Rowand had learned the unfortunate news that the Rev James McLean had never met Admiral Sir Thomas Maitland and the clergyman's signature had been forged. News spread of the grand deception carried out by the impersonator of Admiral Sir Thomas Maitland. All the while, the dinner for two at the Eagle Inn lay on the table going cold. The man in black had gone.

So who was he? The hunt was on. Theories circulated by word-of-mouth and in newspaper columns as to the likely identity of the individual who had shown considerable daring in carrying out his act of fraud. Thoughts turned to reports that back in July 1817 a young man had managed to procure from a Glasgow bank the astonishing amount of £1,314 by means of bills forged with the name of Adamson and Logan, Manufacturers. In a curious twist he had anonymously sent back £900 of this sum in an envelope, and it was suggested that he had found himself unable to dispose of such a large sum. A man of similar youthful looks had attempted to defraud the Waterloo Fund, which had been established to make payments to wounded soldiers. A man identified as Perthshire native Lachlan Stewart was apprehended and held in Edinburgh, but the case never went to trial. Accounts later appeared in the press that the same individual had undertaken a swindling tour of the north under the assumed names of Colonel or Captain Stewart of Uphall.

In January the following year, an unidentified young man claiming to be from Rosshire had popped up at Dunvegan in Skye, and acted with an unknown accomplice to obtain goods and payments from a bank fund. It didn't come to light that the fund was fictitious until after he had gone. In February 1819 a crime took place that could be seen as a practise run for the Ship Bank fraud. In the village of Methven an elegant gig pulled up and out stepped a person who declared himself to be a gentleman belonging to one of the banks in nearby Perth. The gentleman took up quarters at the Barossa Inn, where the landlady ordered clean sheets for the bed and complied with his every want. One morning he made it known that he was going to meet someone at the manse of Tippermuir. He asked for a stable boy to accompany him, giving the impression that he intended to return for dinner. But when the gig reached a quiet part of the road the man performed the ungentlemanly act of pushing the boy out of the vehicle and driving away with it. The stable boy managed to recover his wits and gave chase as far as Bridge of Earn where, thoroughly out of puff, he was forced to give up.

Clearly the fraudulent Admiral had a colourful past. The authorities were determined to catch him. By the end of the day of his profitable visit to the Ship Bank, police officers were searching the streets of Glasgow, but he must have fled that part of the country. Little progress was made until 1st November, when the sheriff substitute at Glasgow began to piece together bits of information received. The procurator fiscal at Inverness was on the lookout for one Donald Davidson, a thirty-two-year-old veteran of the Napoleonic wars who was believed to be behind the notorious Captain or Colonel Stewart imposture in the Highlands; a man answering the description of Davidson was known to have travelled to Glasgow by the Highlander steamboat before the Admiral Maitland deception took place; the procurator fiscal at Benbecula believed that Davidson the forger was now somewhere on the islands of South Uist. The Glasgow fiscal sent a man in pursuit. Having learned that the law was on his trail, the fraudster quickly set off to Lochmaddy for the steam packet. After some days of pursuit he was at last caught, apparently hoping to flee to the north by the Caledonian Canal. Davidson was taken to Inverness Prison, then transferred to the tollbooth at Glasgow.

James Haldane, a Glasgow engraver, was called on as a handwriting expert. Comparing the writing on Admiral Maitland's draft with letters previously written by the prisoner, he concluded that they were by the same person. The identity of the forger having been established, firm evidence was sought that he had left his island home and travelled to Glasgow at the time of the crime. Davidson refuted this. In a statement he said that in the days before the crime was committed he had been at Fort William collecting his war pension and proceeded home from there on a sloop called the Ann Shaw. He protested strongly that although the Ann Shaw stopped at Crinan, he did not travel eastwards to Glasgow through the Crinan Canal. He had gone directly to South Uist. As for a steamboat called the Highlander, he swore that he had never heard of such a vessel.

However, the steward of the Highlander steam boat was in a position to gainsay that. Not only had the prisoner come aboard at Fort William, he said, but he had remained on the vessel through the locks of the Crinan Canal and all the way to the Broomielaw in Glasgow. The steward was brought to the tollbooth, where he identified Davidson. The forger exclaimed: "I'm done for now." To make matters worse for him, another witness came forward. Norman McDonald, a seaman on the Ann Shaw, had seen Davidson on his vessel in early November; in other words, the forger hadn't made a clean getaway from Glasgow after all. MacDonald had seen Davidson board at Lochgilphead and travel westwards through the Crinan Canal en route to Benbecula.

The trial took place in April 1822. While in custody Davidson continued to test the authorities. He made a complaint about poor hygiene in his cell so that he could get a fresh set of clothes and he managed somehow to alter his appearance so that when some of the witnesses took the stand, they were unsure as to whether this was the same person. The most eminent witness to attend was the real Admiral Sir Thomas Maitland, who was currently his Majesty's Lord High Commissioner. During the trial, details of Davidson's eventful life began to emerge. He was the son of a military man based at Fort George and had grown up in the Inverness area with his three brothers. With his father and brothers he had served for some years in the 95th (Rifles) Regiment of Foot, a regiment unusual in encouraging literacy even among the lower ranks. The role was likely to demand a firmness of nerve, as its men would often go out as skirmishers in front of the main body of soldiers. Davidson had participated in a particularly bloody chapter of the peninsular wars, the storming of the Fortress of Badajoz in April 1812.

It's believed that some of Davidson's regiment had been part of a forlorn hope, meaning that the majority were not expected to survive the assault. Prospects were little better for those coming up behind, who faced a barrage of musket fire as they struggled to clamber over a wall of slain bodies that continually grew in height. Davidson's expectations of survival would have been slim. Within a few hours 4,800 allied soldiers had been killed, 382 from Davidson's regiment, and countless more injured. What happened next became notorious. The surviving British soldiers got very drunk and rampaged through the town in a three-day orgy that saw the massacre of thousands of Spanish civilians. In the midst of all this carnage and chaos, Davidson had lost his lower left arm and he was pensioned off in 1813.

It isn't recorded how Davidson was affected psychologically by participating in the storming of Badajoz. In addition to the amputation of his lower arm, he is likely to have borne less visible scars. It's possible that he developed a devil-may-care attitude or an appetite for risk-taking that equipped him for the role of fraudster, and perhaps his period of service stirred a certain admiration for eminent military men. He was the stereotype of the broken soldier, having returned from conflict at a young age with a missing limb and a dramatic story, and left reliant on the imperfect Chelsea out-pension system for war veterans. Evidence suggests that men who returned from the Napoleonic wars with injuries were not necessarily greeted as heroes and some may have turned to crime. After leaving the Rifles, Davidson took up civilian life by marrying a native of South Uist and starting a family in Upper Bornish.

Among the many witnesses called to give evidence against him was Robert McDonald of the Highlander, who said that the accused had managed to conceal his missing arm throughout the journey on the steamboat. By making alterations in his appearance while in prison, Davidson did manage to flummox some of the witnesses, but this trickery would not save him from the machinery of justice. The jury unanimously returned a guilty verdict with a recommendation to mercy, partly on the grounds of having lost his arm in the service of his country. The judge, however, sentenced the forger to be hanged on 29th May. He appealed the sentence, on the basis of his good army service and that his wife and children would be plunged into penury and despair; and in a final burst of defiance, he claimed this had been his first offence. His sentence was reduced to transportation for life. In August 1822 he was transferred to Woolwich, where he would remain aboard the prison hulk Justitia for six months, in chains and put to hard labour. On 18th March 1823 he set sail on the Competitor with 160 other convicts, bound for Van Diemen's Land. This episode shows how an inhabitant of the Highlands and Islands could turn the tables and show considerable ingenuity and daring in committing a crime in the Lowlands.

Terror Aboard the Justicia

For one diminutive Highlander the Union Canal would forever be associated with a terrifying ordeal he suffered at the hands of four young boatmen. Hector Black was visiting the town of Linlithgow in the autumn of 1837. A tailor by trade, Black carried the needle case and thimbles of his trade and modest earnings. Although the testimonies given by the accused boatmen would vary in respect of a few details, there is no doubt that they kidnapped Black, held him for several hours and pressed him to hand over his money on pain of his life. He was a long way from his home in Ardnamurchan, a part of Scotland still noted for its remoteness. Ardnamurchan hadn't benefited from the road-making that had opened up other districts of the Highlands, leaving the area reliant on a single-track road for communication with the rest of the country. Black lodged with a tenant farmer in Kilmory, a small crofting township on the coast. Despite the great distances and physical discomforts, temporary migration to the Lowlands was then increasingly a recognised feature between May and September when food scarcity was at its greatest.

Black's journey to the central belt was almost certainly a matter of necessity rather than choice, owing to the desperate conditions in his native parish and in the Highlands generally. By the late 1830s a number of factors had plunged the inhabitants from surviving at subsistence level into near-famine in many districts. The population had been rising for decades, putting increasing pressure on small parcels of land and stretching supplies of the potato, which was the mainstay of the diet. The landowner in Black's home territory was Sir James Riddell, whose estate had been losing money since the 1820s. The kelping industry, with which some inhabitants of the area supplemented their meagre living, faced collapse. In seeking ways to turn his land to profit, Riddell's thinking turned to the doctrine known as Improvement, which was fashionable with the influential classes. In the Ardnamurchan area boundaries were redrawn and communities cleared so that Cheviot sheep could be brought in to raise revenue. The households targeted for removal were the poorest and judgements on the perceived moral shortcomings of individuals were also taken into account. People from neighbouring clachans were resettled in Kilmory. In Hector Black's parish the potato crop had only just sufficed to keep the inhabitants alive these past five years. In 1837, Home Office agent Robert Graham was told by the local minister that the poorest of the parish were considerably more destitute than in previous years because of the failure of the kelping, two years of poor weather and the subdivision of land into parcels far too small for the inhabitants to live on.

Hector Black was in Linlithgow on the night of Sunday, 17th September. In addition to the sewing materials he carried, he had earnings of twenty-six shillings in a purse. Just before midnight he ascended one of the steep wynds leading away from the town's warm hostelries, carrying a knife, a purse containing a small sum and the needle and sewing case needed for his trade. He reached the canal basin where coal boat No. 25, the Justitia, had been lying idle all day. A distinguishing feature of this crew was its youthfulness. Master Charles Stewart was twenty and he had engaged seventeen-year-old Arthur Corner, the son of a porter, as his driver. Preparing to leave with them were the sixteen-year-olds Alexander MacArthur, a farm servant at Kettilstoun, Linlithgow, and Edinburgh man John Bruce, who went by the ominous nickname of 'Punch Bruce' or "Punch Palmer".

Black was standing on the bridge at the Linlithgow basin, puffing on his pipe, when events quickly ran out of his control. A man snatched the pipe from his mouth and began walking towards the coal boat with it. Black started after him to recover it and as they drew level with the vessel, the man seized his arms and pitched him into the boat. Black managed to get himself upright and ashore, but the assailant pursued him and again shoved him into the Justitia, which was immediately pushed off from the side. In less than a minute the tailor had been taken captive on the boat, whose driver and horses now pushed inexorably through the darkness towards the Avon aqueduct. Black was compelled to enter the cabin where the three other crew men were drinking, and pressed a whisky on the Highlander, as they insisted on calling him. The drink was no sooner in his hand than Alexander MacArthur had knocked it to the ground and begun angrily demanding payment for the cost of the broken glass. Black replied he hadn't enough money and pleaded to be allowed ashore. The boat drifted on, with Charles Stewart declaring that Black must hand over two shillings as his fare. Stewart, McArthur and Bruce expressed disbelief when the man protested that he had no money, so they forced him to take off his jacket and vest and trousers. The men became increasingly volatile and one of them, Corner or Bruce, grabbed a poker and threatened to knock the captive's brains out. The terrified Black called out "Murder!" and his attempts to get off the boat were thwarted by Stewart.

Some time later the master relented and allowed him to go ashore. On reaching the bank, the tailor began to declare loudly that he had been robbed. This was a mistake, because it provoked Stewart into disembarking and threatening to drown him into silence. Black was by this time in a state of sheer terror and had little idea where he was. His jacket was in his hand and the neck cloth he'd been wearing earlier had disappeared. But help was at hand, and Black's ordeal was coming to a close. The four men were apprehended and imprisoned at the tollbooth in Linlithgow. They were charged with forcing Black onto the boat, assaulting him and robbing him of twenty-six shillings, a purse, a clasp knife, neck cloth, a needle case and thimbles. The four pled not guilty. The trial took place in March 1838 at the High Court in Edinburgh.

Stewart gave a statement exonerating himself from all blame and going as far as to cast himself in the role of the peacemaker. He claimed that he had been at the helm when the journey began and dozed for much of the time. He was wakened, he said, by the breaking out of a disturbance between the Highlander and MacArthur and Palmer. Stewart had thought to calm the situation, he claimed, by putting the passenger ashore east of the Avon aqueduct. He swore that at no point in the journey did he see Black with any clothes missing and he denied refusing to let the tailor leave the boat. The master also claimed that he had got onto the bank to assist Black. Stewart had heard the tailor calling out that he had been robbed, and claimed that the crime had been carried out close to the Avon Aqueduct by a father and son named George and Alexander Nimmo, who were then passing on their vessel. Stewart also attempted to pin the blame on MacArthur and Palmer, saying that they had stolen three shillings and sixpence from his waistcoat pocket during the course of that night, and he'd gone off to try and find them.

The court was not swayed by the denials of Stewart and his crew men. The four were found guilty and sentenced to 14 years transportation. Stewart appealed for clemency, saying that MacArthur and Bruce had committed the crime while he was asleep at the helm. He also pointed out that he had a wife and family dependent on him and he suffered from a fistula. Not only did his plea for sympathy fall on deaf ears, but it resulted in his separation from the other three. Stewart set sail on the Coromandel in June and arrived in Van Diemen's Land, now Tasmania, in the October of that year. Bruce, Corner and MacArthur arrived in Australia on the Earl Grey the following month.

Canal-Making Conflict in the Highlands

Trouble had been brewing on the Highland canals even when they were in the making, partly on account of the influx of 'strangers' into parts of the country where people were naturally wary of incomers. In the early 1800s nearly 1000 men were working on Thomas Telford's ambitious Caledonian Canal. Telford had had a number of tradesmen brought north from the Ellesmere Canal in Wales, where they had acquired considerable technical experience and expertise. As far as the Scottish natives were concerned, Welsh was synonymous with English. Among the Welsh contingent was Thomas Davies, who proved to be a valued contractor. Davies had come north with his teenage son John, a mild-mannered young man who would be learning on the job. For Thomas Davies things were going well. In 1804 he had begun work at Kinmylies with ten men and by the close of that year his workforce had grown to 123. By 1814 Davies Senior and Junior were living at Fort Augustus and work on the locks with masons and blacksmiths was going on.

But life became difficult for the mild-mannered John Davies. His quiet nature had attracted the attention of a bully who was seeking prey, and who may have resented incomers. The bully in question was James Cummings, the son of a local blacksmith who was working on the canal. Cummings was in the habit of calling John Davies names and his favourite sport was trying to goad him into acts of retaliation. On one fateful occasion Cummings incited Davies and he got his way: he succeeded in escalating the ill-feeling to a fist fight. Amid the scuffle, Davies broke free. He grabbed hold of a stone which he threw at Cummings' head. Cummings got up and ran after Davies, knocked him down and beat him hard so that he was bleeding. But the blow to the Cumming's head from the stone been more serious than either of them realised. Cummings fell down and had to be carried home. He lay in a stupor for ten hours and after that nothing could be done to revive him. He passed away.

On 21st September John Davies was charged with having killed James Cummings. The case was treated as culpable homicide because it had quickly emerged from the evidence that Cummings was "continually persecuting" Davies. Lord Meadowbank, in summing up the case, said he did not believe that Davies intended serious injury to the deceased, though he could not be regarded as entirely free of blame. The jury found him guilty but recommended to him to mercy. This meant that they were signalling to the judge that they did not believe he should be hanged. The judge responded by handing down the unusually lenient sentence for culpable homicide of 40 days. John Davies was helped by general interest in his predicament, and there had been clear public sympathy towards him as a victim of bullying. Many a bully gets away with it—but Cummings paid with his life.

Trouble was not long in breaking out during the making of the Crinan Canal, which began in 1794. Masons, blacksmiths, boat makers and joiners were few and far between in the area before work began; and men of these specialised trades often had to eke out a living by undertaking humble labouring work such as making ditches and fences. In the *Old Statistical Account* of 1794, a portrait-of-the-nation survey compiled by clergymen, it was noted that people of this part of the world were mild and docile in character and the clergyman doubted whether any other parish in Scotland would have such a low incidence of crime. It would be only five years later that a violent incident took place in which, as with the fatal fight between Cummings and Davies on the Caledonian, a history of personal animosity played its part. It began on a February night when mason William Morris was walking along the road between Kilmichael and Lochgilphead.

A man jumped out of the shadows and began setting about Morris with a bayonet. Morris was struck on the head and body many times over. He was so badly wounded that the medic who attended him, Dr Alexander MacArthur of Kilmichael, feared that he wouldn't pull through. The trial didn't take place until the December of that year, to allow Morris to recover from his ordeal. The accused was a local man, Charles Campbell of Craigmurrel. Dr MacArthur and two fellow masons, Peter McEwan and John Cleghorn, appeared as witnesses, as did the local innkeeper. It emerged that that Campbell had long borne a grudge against his victim or, as the judge called it, "a deadly malice," and the calculated nature of the attack was revealed by the fact that the attacker had lain in wait. Campbell was sentenced to one month's imprisonment and payment of a fine binding him to keep the peace in future. Given the ferocity of the assault and the fact that the victim had nearly died, this was a remarkably lenient punishment. Presumably there was a wider context to this turn of events, which the history books have yet to reveal. Certainly, this was a turbulent time for an area that had seen few changes for centuries: more than thirty tenants in the area had been with eviction notices to clear the area for sheep and others still were displaced from their homes by the making of the canal.

CHAPTER SIX: RUTHLESS TRADERS

Burke, Hare and the Mysterious Mr Ironson

Scotland's canals have played their part in the murky history of resurrectionism, though the full extent of the trade in canal-borne cadavers will never be known. Newspapers from the first half of the nineteenth century feature hundreds of accounts of men spotted disturbing fresh plots at graveyards in almost every part of the country. Some bereaved families camped out by their loved one's resting place, equipped with big sticks and guns, and perhaps a bottle of whisky to help them through the weary vigils that might go on for two weeks or more. In social and criminal terms bodysnatchers were viewed by the public as the dregs of humanity, not least because their financial motivation was stirred by someone else's loss. Outwardly respectable medical men might also be active participants. There was steady demand for stolen corpses at all of Scotland's medical schools, since only the bodies of hanged criminals were available through official channels for the demonstration of anatomy. The prestigious school at Edinburgh would pay up to £10 for a corpse in good condition—far more than a labourer could earn in a month. A blind eye was often turned to the question of where the bodies had come from, since anatomy demonstrations were a mandatory part of a surgeon's training. A shady-looking character could turn up at the back door with a 'subject' or 'thing' in a barrel, confident that he would be paid with no questions asked.

From the 1820s, rumours grew that the Forth and Clyde and the Union Canal had become major transport routes for corpses bound the Glasgow and Edinburgh medical schools. In time it became clear that there was no smoke without fire. An iron-goods company, Redpath and Brown, was doing a great trade in mortsafes. Particular precautions were taken in graveyards adjacent to the banks. At Cadder Parish Church, close to the Forth and Clyde, a tower was built to accommodate night-time watchers, and mortsafes—iron cages protecting a grave—were in use. Muiravonside Parish Church was so close to the Union Canal that part of the ground had been lost to the excavation. Even before the waterway fully open, it was claimed that boatmen lifted bodies from Muiravonside onto an east-bound barge; the location was just too convenient. At Linlithgow several incidents occurred in the churchyard the year after the canal was finished. It is not clear whether the disinterred were transported to Edinburgh by road; the road was closer to the churchyard, but the canal would have been more discreet.

Reports of body-snatching activity in Scotland are often based on anecdote, speculation and rumour. Perhaps the most inaccurate myths concern William Burke and William Hare, the Irishmen who crossed the sea with hundreds of their compatriots and dug the Union Canal. It is often said, particularly in tourist and heritage publications, that the duo dug up bodies and transported them to Edinburgh for sale, but there is no evidence to support this. During the years of the Union's excavation, Burke and Hare undertook the exhausting toil of canal digging. After this steady work finished in 1822 the pair scrabbled around for any work they could find—Hare worked as a lumber, or boat-loader, at Port Hopetoun for the coal agent James Dawson, Burke dabbled at shoe-mending, and both picked up work in sheep-shearing, among other things. The serious illness of a lodger at Hare's house inspired the pair to embark on a profitable career of smothering vulnerable people to death, so that the bodies could be sold to Dr Knox at Edinburgh's medical school. Burke and Hare were prolific serial killers, not resurrection men; and they used roads rather than canals to move their human cargo. Burke once disposed of a victim's clothing in the Union Canal. This was an unwise thing to do and it was perhaps inevitable that the pair, becoming increasingly emboldened, would arouse suspicions and be reported to the police. Only Burke and his common-law-wife Nellie McDougal were charged with murder. Hare gave evidence against his erstwhile friend with his wife Margaret—a tough woman who had been one of the tiny minority of female canal labourers. The Hares had to flee an angry mob following the trial. McDougal was found not proven and Burke was hanged in January, 1829 before a crowd estimated to be as large as 20,000.

Three years prior to the execution of William Burke, a sensational operation in corpse-trading on Scotland's canals had been discovered. The Latona incident provided firm evidence of goings-on that were suspected for years. The ensuing investigation exposed the astonishing scale of operations and the ambitious distances that corpse-traders were prepared to transport their unsavoury cargo. In October of 1826 the Latona, a vessel owned by the Carron Company of Grangemouth, was berthed at Liverpool docks. The crew was getting ready to sail north, then along the Forth and Clyde, when they began to notice something amiss. A foul stench was coming from cargo they were stowing aboard. They traced the smell to a shipment of three casks marked "Bitter Salts" with an accompanying note signed J Brown requesting that they be sent to a Mr G H Ironson, Edinburgh. The unenviable task of examining the cargo fell to Captain Walker, who pulled some straw out of a hole. The stench was growing unbearable, but he bravely inserted a hand inside the cask. He realised that this was a cargo of dead bodies that were beginning to decay. He contacted the local agent for the Carron Company, who in turn informed the police.

Officer Robert Boughey attended the Latona and found that a carter named George Leech, had brought the casks to the quay from the city's Hope Street. Boughey summoned other officers and had Leech lead them to a cellar in Hope Street, which lay beneath the school room of a Rev. MacGowan. MacGowan said he had no key to the room, since he had rented it to a John Henderson of Greenock, who had said he was a cooper. The police took a crowbar to the door and entered to find a house of horror inside. Cadavers were hidden in four casks and three sacks, along with a syringe of the sort anatomists used to inject hot wax into the veins of bodies. Also, there was a collection of clothes that were probably intended to be used as disguises by the criminal gang. A surgeon, Thomas William Davis, then had to open the casks and sacks found aboard the Latona and in the cellar. In total, Davies counted thirty-three bodies—men, women and children. Finding no marks of violence on them, he concluded that they must have been unearthed from burying grounds in the Liverpool area. Some had been dead two or three days; others, six or seven. Judging from the materials found in the cellar, such as a large brass syringe, they had been injected with preservative liquid, pickled in brine, then packed in dry salt with the purpose of staving off the process of putrefaction.

The mayor, town clerk and other officials swiftly moved to investigate. It was established that, despite precautions taken at the town's parish cemetery, bodies had been exhumed there. It was becoming apparent that Henderson had been a false name. Leech described having been approached by a tall, stout man with dark whiskers and a Scottish accent. The man asked how much he would charge to cart three casks from Hope Street to the George's Dock Passage. When Leech arrived in the street, two men were manhandling the casks out of the cellar. They gave him the shipping note, paid him the fee, and tipped him extra to "be careful" in putting the casks down on the quay—perhaps an attempt to buy Leech's silence. A couple named Hindley and another woman gave information that led to the arrest the Scotsman. James Donaldson, regarded as the gang's ringleader, was found to possess incriminating shipping notes. Before the month was out he had been tried and imprisoned for twelve months. His Scottish fellow lodgers, Peter MacGregor and John Mack, were apprehended soon afterwards following botched attempts to send bodies to Edinburgh by road.

The Union Canal Conspiracy

In Stockbridge, Edinburgh, a street is named after Captain Alexander Cheyne, the man who was appointed clerk to the Union Canal Company in March 1823. Cheyne was the second person to occupy of this influential administrative position and given his impeccable credentials his should have been a safe appointment. Shortly after he took up the post he began to introduce changes, however, which set alarm bells ringing with some of the company's employees. Step by step he propelled the Union Canal into an extraordinary crisis which worried and angered some of his underlings. Within three years of the waterway's opening, the Captain's activities had set the company finances on course for ruin as he unleashed one the most ambitious fraudulent schemes of early nineteenth century Scotland. Like all the best financial scandals, it was hushed up—until now.

In early 1822, the Union Canal's clerk, Cheyne's predecessor, was George Moncreiff. A formidable man from an eminent legal family, Moncrieff was appointed when the canal was still only a proposal. He threw himself into campaigning for legal permission to construct the waterway, then put his shoulder to the often-frustrating task of administering its construction. While the waterway nearing completion the cost of its excavation soared far above the engineer's estimate. Hugh Baird's anxieties about the safety of his great aqueducts, technical problems with the tunnel at Prospect Hill in Falkirk, wayward contractors and grasping landowners were all taking their toll on the bill. The company urgently needed to get the waterway open, since profits from charging tolls could only be reaped once boats were plying east and west. Gangs of navvies were seen working in a frenzy, shovelling earth and wheeling barrows by torchlight. As time went on, Moncrieff had become heavy-handed in his treatment of contractors he saw as lazy. He had heel-dragging contractors sacked and seized their 'lots' for direct management under the company. He grew increasingly annoyed with landowners who were determined to squeeze every penny they could get in compensation for the loss of land. Despite all the adversity, in March 1822 the waterway was on track to be finished within two months.

Then, on March 15th, disaster struck. At his grand rented house in the Canongate, Moncrieff died from an episode recorded as apoplexy—a sudden loss of consciousness followed by death, perhaps caused by a stroke. It was a terrible blow for his wife, a genteel poet named Frances, who was left to bring up young daughters; and for the canal company the first clerk's death was catastrophic. It opened a huge hole in the daily running of the business and left them wondering who they could look to for help. The engineer, Hugh Baird, wasn't in a position to take on much more work. Baird had brought up three children on his own, ran a small family farm near Kilsyth and, now in his forties, was engineer to both the Forth of Clyde and the Union Canals. For years he had been horse-riding across more than 60 miles of rough country, attempting to placate cantankerous landowners and being lowered into muddy holes deep in the ground. His family involvement in the political turmoil of the Scottish Insurrection of 1820 took a further toll. By the time of Moncrieff's demise Baird was physically and mentally depleted. The canal opened for business in May 1822 without a hint of the official ceremony that would have taken place had Moncrieff been alive. A boat loaded with flagstones left Edinburgh and that was it.

Enter Alexander Cheyne, armed with several gushing testimonials, in response to an advert for clerk. Thirty-eight-year-old Cheyne came from a large family with respectable connections in medicine and the law. He had begun working life apprenticed to an iron founder in Lanarkshire, then joined the Royal Engineers, who promoted him to captain after distinguished service during the Peninsular War. He retired on half-pay, meaning he could take up employment on condition that he would be ready to resume full active service if a major conflict blew up. Even at that early stage, one of the canal's proprietor perceived a mercenary streak in Cheyne. The proprietor wrote an anonymous letter to the *Caledonian Mercury* arguing that Cheyne could only make a serious commitment to the clerkship if he gave up the half-pay. But Cheyne was not the sort to let a disgruntled pen-wielder get in his way. In a published reply he tore into his 'anonymous assailant,' accusing him of ignorance and asserting he had every right to the job.

In March 1823, Cheyne took his place in the office at Port Hopetoun, Edinburgh, on a salary of £300 per annum, one-third more than the engineer's pay. A few weeks later the committee advised its 26 employees that they must obey all Cheyne's orders and show him proper respect, subject to committee approval—an instruction that looks like the promise of things to come. One way to ensure compliance was to get rid of anyone who might potentially stand in his way. A clue as to what the new clerk was getting up to at that early stage can be gleaned by looking at recruitment adverts in the newspapers. On two of the company's passage boats the position of boatmaster had become vacant. On a further two other vessels, a mate and two new stewards were required. In May, the company appealed for candidates for another boatman. By early autumn the position of head lock-keeper on the Union Canal had become vacant. The toll collector at Linlithgow also needed replacing. For so many workers to leave within a short space of time was extraordinary. The explanation lay with what Cheyne had been doing behind the scenes. He had been dismissing numerous company servants, usually without consulting the committee. The first lot to go had been Master William Benson of the Flora McIvor, Master John Scott of the Bailie Nicol Jarvie, and two mates and a steward from the Alexander. There was an apparent explanation that went with these dismissals, though it isn't clear how true it was. One day in April, the story went, the master of the Alexander had fallen sick and Scott took charge. The Alexander met Benson's boat and Benson, clearly the worse for drink, came aboard. Scott had allowed the behaviour of Benson, the other crew members and some passengers to get out of hand. Hence the advert to replace these men insisted the candidates must demonstrate their integrity, sobriety and attention to duty.

Next to be shown the door was Master Henry Johnston of the Jeanie Deans, who claimed he had been dismissed for no reason. In October John Broom, the head lock-keeper, had been sent away without any instruction from the committee. The highest profile victim of the attrition was the Linlithgow collector John Greig, a man who had been associated with the canal from its earliest days. Cheyne had dismissed Greig merely because his name had featured on a handbill for Murray's Luggage Boat Service. The accusation was that Greig had been moonlighting, breaking the rule that servants should work for the canal company and no one else. However, the dismissal was unjust. It was well known that Greig had neither acted as an agent for Murray's, nor received any payment from them. An outcry ensued, and as a result he was reinstated as collector. Rather than rebuke Cheyne for his overzealous action, the committee gave him mild advice as to how he should exercise his authority. It seems that the Captain had got quite a hold on them. In March, 1824 he persuaded them to give him an award of expenses on top of his salary. The following year he was seeking a further pay rise. He warned the company that he might have to leave the position of clerk since the Royal Engineers were on the point of re-engaging him. This threat to leave them in the lurch had the desired effect, as it secured him a top-up of £200 per annum—at the expense of Hugh Baird, whose pay was cut by the same amount. Baird's health was variable by 1824. However, there was no doubt that he was working for the canal company. He had rented a house in George Street, Edinburgh, to enable him to attend to teething problems such as low water levels. He also acted as consulting engineer on maintenance works and in the planning of a railway for canal-borne coal. The committee declared its deep satisfaction with Baird's "zealous and able manner," but this praise is likely to have rung hollow with the engineer. The pay-cut contributed to the financial difficulties he faced in his final years. On his death in 1827, his sons and daughter were left in debt.

In return for the pay increase for Cheyne, it was stipulated that the clerk must undertake to give the canal his undivided attention during the office hours of 10am and 4pm. The phrase "undivided attention" suggests that someone had suggested to the committee that the Captain might be spending too much time somewhere else. Indeed he was spending too much of his time somewhere else, and this was ironic given his treatment of John Greig for alleged moonlighting. When he was supposed to be at the office at Port Hopetoun, Cheyne was often to be found in Stockbridge, inspecting the great property development that was helping to enrich him. As recently as the 1810s, this part of Edinburgh had been a patchwork of fields, orchards and country lanes dotted with a minimal smattering of houses. The early 1820s saw the area transformed through development. Cart-loads of wood and stone arrived daily for the squads of labourers, masons, carpenters and plumbers who were at work building houses, shops and roads. By February 1825, shops and houses of varying sizes had been completed and were ready for purchase or rent. The *Scots Magazine* in 1826 said: "This flourishing village is extending more rapidly than any other suburb of Edinburgh." Cheyne had launched himself as a property developer the year in 1822 and after he became canal clerk his involvement went on unabated, contrary to the company's rules. Witnesses later said that Cheyne left the canal office about six or seven times a day, and in time the hours he spent haunting the growing buildings of Stockbridge became a bone of contention with the canal committee. To add to the intrigue, his involvement in Stockbridge was swathed in secrecy. Adverts for the properties never mentioned him by name, but directed interested parties were to speak to a Mr James Shillinglaw.

The Captain's extensive property development, comprising more than fifty houses, was only the start of his ambitions. Far from giving the canal his undivided attention, he began from the year 1825 to throw himself into an array of business speculations. He took full advantage of the opening of a second canal basin named Port Hamilton. Port Hamilton had been constructed close to Port Hopetoun in order to accommodate the increasing numbers of boats loading and unloading. A group of key merchants had held berths and offices at Port Hopetoun ever since the canal opened. There they sold their wares to the public and supplied the canal company with coal for its own boats. However, Captain Cheyne began ordering the traders to vacate their premises at Port Hopetoun and insisted that they move to the new basin, which was less convenient for trade. The Duke of Hamilton's agent, James Dawson, protested that at Port Hamilton he would miss out on passing trade from Lothian Road, but Cheyne insisted that his office was needed by a firm of stone merchants named Kerr and Baxter. Dawson suspected that this Kerr and Baxter had been enlisted for the sole purpose of ousting him. Relations worsened when the canal company eschewed Dawson and began getting its own coal from a new source with a familiar name—a supplier by the name of James Shillinglaw.

Cheyne's dealings were certainly shadowy, but they hadn't gone unnoticed. At this point a further cloak-and-dagger twist took place.

A member of the canal committee, Andrew Paton, strongly believed that the clerk was up to something and decided to start seeking evidence. Discreetly Paton approached the canal's western overseer, John Easton, and recruited him as a spy to keep watch on Cheyne. Easton's task was to note in a journal everywhere the Captain went, who he met and what his dealings were. In particular, Paton wanted a record of how much time the Captain was spending on canal business. The journal, which spanned from August 1825 to mid-1826, would reveal that Easton was an appalling speller but a first-rate spy. In great detail he documented the Captain's rapid and often convoluted movements. His entries often concluded with the damning phrase: "Little or no canal business done."

The Captain was a busy man—though seldom with canal duties. On many occasions he got into his boat at Port Hopetoun with his trusty dog and set out westwards. Starting in the small hours not only allowed him to be discreet, it also enabled him to pack as much as possible into his day, and there is no doubt that he was an impatient man. He was accompanied on these trips by a retinue of canal company servants—a boy to drive the horses that pulled the boat, the eastern overseer George Beeby, Port Hopetoun office porter John Lambert and a lock-keeper or bank maintenance man. He required these people to carry his bag and gun and wait on him while he participated in his favourite past-times of pheasant shooting and fox hunting. One diary entry, for November 11th 1825, offers a taste of the Captain's busy schedule. John Easton, the spy, was able to recall that day vivid detail not least because it featured a waterborne collision. Just after 4am the Captain's boat set off from Port Hopetoun and Cheyne settled into his hammock for an extended snooze. The company boy had driven the horses through Linlithgow and just beyond the town the Captain was rudely awakened by a great jolt. The impact almost threw him out of the hammock and tipped items off the table onto the floor. It turned out that Cheyne's vessel had been struck by the night boat going in the other direction. No one was hurt, fortunately, and once the travellers had dusted themselves off the journey was resumed. A while later the Captain rose and spruced himself up. First appointment of the day was at Glenfuir, Falkirk, with the stonemason James Wyse, who had supervised the construction of the canal's eleven locks. Easton's entry is clear that official canal business was far down the agenda. The Captain wanted to discuss with Wyse a malting enterprise that he wanted to get up and running. That done, Cheyne "took a turn across the tunnel with his gun" before the party headed eastwards to what may have well been the Captain's favourite happy hunting ground, Preston Field.

The estate, bordering the canal at the western end of Linlithgow, was owned by Dr Seton, an influential baron of the realm. In the nineteenth century the estate was extensive. Species populations in the area were then plentiful and included deer, foxes, wildfowl and birds of prey but faced threats from the ambitions of men—not unlike today's swans, bats and badgers, which have to contend with ongoing canalside development. In Cheyne's time, custodians of the land could profit via the Linlithgow and Stirlingshire Hunt. This club of wealthy gentlemen shared bloodlust and the ambition to form advantageous social and business connections. Members included the fabulously wealthy William Forbes of Callendar. On the day of the boating accident Easton described, Cheyne hunted at Preston until 5 o'clock in the evening. On another occasion, a passing puppy out for a walk on the estate excitedly joined in the hunt. The pup ran with the hounds until it managed to get the fox's head in its small jaws—a gory climax that tickled the gentleman-chums.

To put it mildly, the Captain was not giving the canal his undivided attention. As though this energetic hunting and shooting were not enough, he was carrying out a remarkable number of business enterprises, mainly during the hours when he was supposed to be in the office. In mid-1825, after he had managed to oust the traders from Port Hopetoun, he began trading in stone. It appears that the first stone quarry he took on was at Brightons. Within less than a year he was operating at least five canal-side quarries: Brightons, Haining, Kingscavel, Nicholton and Callendar. The latter was leased from his sporting companion Forbes, a circumstance that particularly maddened Andrew Paton, since that family of landowners was an ongoing thorn in the canal company's side and had cost them a fortune. At Brighton Wharf he outwitted his competitors by piling up stones to block their path, and is said to have remarked: "The sooner the wharf is blocked up altogether, the better." It was in the spring of 1826 that he branched out into coal. He was soon bringing this article from Gartsherrie, Sherriffhall and the north of England. Slate was another speciality. He had a yard at Broxburn and a larger depot at Leith, with further supplies brought in from as far afield as Easdale on the west coast. He also traded in lime, a product used by farmers. As his discussions about malting with James Wyse suggest, he was distilling too, on the banks of Forth and Clyde.

He had his finger in a remarkable number of pies. None of this would have been possible without his position as clerk. The benefit was twofold. He had control of the channel of distribution and had a reserve of manpower and expertise in the shape of company servants: masons, carters, toll collectors and even humble lock-keepers. Testimonies suggest that he was a bully who made his inferiors afraid of challenging him. According to Easton's journal, the servants were often absent from their official duties for hours while they attended his demands. It is difficult to assess the total of Cheyne's illicit trading activities as he generally hid behind the trading name of his private employees, James and Andrew Shillinglaw. One worker at Kingscavel later stated that Cheyne had urged that his own name should not be mentioned in connection with the operation. Both Shillinglaw brothers came regularly to the company office in Edinburgh and were seen in private conversation with the Captain, an array of books and papers spread out before them on the desk. Like a participant in a spy drama, the clerk would place a lighted lamp in the widow as a signal showing it was safe for them to approach.

In summer 1826, the inevitable happened. Cheyne was sued under his own name after some of his coal caused damage to a neighbour's garden; and in a separate incident James Shillinglaw, who was illiterate, gave the game away after he was unable to forge his master's signature on a document. An aggregate committee made up of twelve committee members and twelve proprietors was formed to investigate the company's financial affairs. Evening meetings were held and the evidence began to mount up that Cheyne had been submitting financial reports that were somewhat rosier than the reality. In 1827 an enquiry was launched into how all twenty-six company servants were performing their duties, and the following year "financial embarrassments" were closely examined. After some considerable time, evidence against Cheyne had been gathered up and he stood accused of six main charges: neglecting canal business; operating his own private trades; carrying out these trades under the assumed name of Shillinglaw; employing company servants in this trade and travelling at the company's expense; oppression of other traders on the canal; and charging the company for works done by the Shillinglaws at inflated prices.

Needless to say, the Captain did not take these charges lying down. At first he denied them. He later adapted his defence, saying that he had been carrying on other businesses, but his reason for doing so was to stimulate trade on the canal. He also accused certain committee members of conducting a witch-hunt against him. He claimed that Andrew Paton bore him a long-standing grudge, as he had failed to get a position as a canal collector some years before. Easton's journal, he said, had been written in utter defiance of syntax and orthography, and a printed version produced by his enemies on the committee had transformed it into a smooth and legible work that would support their case. He also alleged that another committee member, a Mr Duncan, was seeking to make a profit out of the endless investigations into his conduct. He claimed that Paton and Duncan regarded him as "a worm to be crushed". Indeed, the feeling against him among committee members was not unanimous; one even described him as a faithful servant. In that regard the aggregate committee was split. Many were growing fearful, moreover, that supporters would desert the canal if the serious allegations and evidence about Cheyne's conduct were made public. It was decided that the affair should be dealt with quietly, without involving the much larger group of proprietors who owned shares in the company.

It is not recorded precisely when the canal company's second clerk realised the game was up. At a general assembly of proprietors on 12th April 1831 he tendered his resignation on the basis that it was the only way to resolve the ongoing disharmony. In 1832, the third canal company clerk, David Kinnaird, was in place and the committee was forced to acknowledge that its debts were far greater than previously reported. Alexander Cheyne ended up very a long way from Stockbridge and Preston Field. He went to Australia, and in time was given responsibilities for roads, bridges and pub works. Perhaps he was able to use a combination of charisma, cunning and dominance that propelled him into positions of trust, and made people afraid to question him. That might go some way to explain why a group of Union Canal company servants, many of whom had proved their physical toughness beyond doubt, participated in the long conspiracy of silence. After a honeymoon period, Captain Cheyne's fate on the other side of the world was not altogether happy. A carriage accident left him with a serious limp and, following a work-related controversy, he never found job security.

Please Spare the Horses

It began with an explosive letter to the *Scotsman*, published in September 1849. The correspondent, who lived close to the Union Canal, had written to express horror at the cruel treatment meted out to the horses that pulled the boats. Presumably for fear of a backlash from powerful commercial interests, the writer dared only to give the initial—C. The Friday before putting pen to paper, C had seen a horse that was half-starved and had seen better days dragging a barge ever so slowly while the young driver lashed him continuously to go at a faster pace. The following day a friend of C had seen a different horse reeling from side to side and the towpath, looking breathless. When challenged, the barge men admitted that their boat was of a kind that really required two horses. The letter ended with a heartfelt plea to the canal company to take action to stop the overworking and ill-treatment of horses. This may have been the first public salvo against what was clearly a pretty regular occurrence.

A Society for the Prevention of Cruelty to Animals had been founded in Edinburgh in 1839, and it is possible that C had had something to do with its formation since the treatment of cart horses was a main plank of the organisation's work. The society would later merge with other groups, formed by concerned residents of cities and towns such as Glasgow and Aberdeen, to become the Scottish Society for the Prevention of Cruelty to Animals that we know today. Prosecutions for cruelty to canal horses began to be reported in the mid-1880s and these cases, generally involving boatmen, tended to be extreme. In 1885 boatmen Thomas Torrance and John Calder were charged with cruel actions that led to an animal's death. The pair were seen forcing a horse to draw a loaded boat along the Union Canal near Ratho Gardens, west of Edinburgh, in the autumn of that year. The horse was so exhausted that it collapsed, was dragged by the rope for a distance of 180 yards, fell while still alive into the canal and taken forward another 500 yards before expiring. There could be no disputing the evidence, so Torrance was fined £2.10 shillings and Calder £2, with the option of a month's imprisonment if they could not pay.

In 1891 the chairman of Glasgow's Society for the Prevention of Cruelty to Animals recounted a case he described as "abominable" in which a canal horse's tongue was cut open by the towing rope. He lamented the fact that the law made clamping down difficult: the owner was only liable to face charges if he or she was present at the time the cruel treatment took place. In 1893 a pair of Glasgow boatmen went on the run after another extreme case came to court. Charles Canning Jr and John Canning were charged for their treatment of a horse on the Forth and Clyde Canal towpath between Kirkintilloch and Auchinstarry. The horse belonged to J and G Hay, ship owners, Port Dundas. Between the Friday evening and Saturday morning the pair were said to have cruelly and repeatedly beaten the horse with a strap and thrown stones at it until a raw wound opened up under the collar. They had also apparently urged the animal to go at an unnecessarily quick place while drawing the empty scow, Flora, until the animal was sweating profusely and became exhausted.

Warrants were granted for the apprehension of the pair.

Cruel treatment of a chestnut horse belonging to the same owners came to court ten years later. Boatmen James Cannon and James McCafferty pled guilty to abusing the horse on the Forth and Clyde Canal near Hillhead Bridge by beating it with a stick. Martin Cartwright, the witness who had reported the incident, said he had seen the pair taking turns of thrashing the horse "in a most unmerciful manner", with what seemed to be a whip handle. The tow rope had broken several times, so that the horse plunged through a hedge and down an embankment. Mr Gray, animal cruelty inspector, echoed these details in his report on the case. McCafferty asserted that the horse had not been injured. He claimed that they had been given a horse that was not adequate to the job. It was old, he said, and more experienced boatmen would have known not to accept a horse as old as that in the first place. The sitting magistrate had views on the treatment of horses. He told those present that for over twenty years he had worked in an office that overlooked the canal towing path and that in studying the behaviour of the horses and men, he had come to the conclusion that the horse was easily the nobler of the two; though at the same time, he would not allow his general observations to prejudice the case. The magistrate dismissed the accused's excuses, taking the view that the boatmen had clearly and unnecessarily abused the animal, and issued a fine.

By the early 1900s, nobody could deny that the ill-treatment of horses, without which canal traders couldn't operate, was a regular occurrence. Ignoring injuries, over-driving—the practice of working a horse too hard—and the closely-related racing of canal horses were among the forms of cruelty seen. A woman named Isabella Morrison was charged in 1908, along with a man named William Lang. On the towpath of the Monkland Canal at Coatbridge they drove a horse that was suffering from open sores on each shoulder and under the collar. Lang claimed that he had brought in this horse to replace another horse that was tired. The injured horse had been kept in for ten days to heal its wounds, but this small amount of exercise had led to the sores reopening. However a police officer had seen blood oozing from below the collar as the animal was going along the canal and had noted that it was clearly in great pain. A penalty of 15 shillings or five days imprisonment was imposed by the sheriff.

George Campbell, a horse driver who lived in Grangemouth, was the accused in a 1910 case that highlighted the practice of boats racing one another to get to the canal locks. What was said at the hearing made it clear that mistreatment was depressingly commonplace. Campbell was riding the horse he was mistreating. He had little hope of getting away with it since there were numerous witnesses, including one who had particular responsibility for animal cruelty. It was clear that by this time the tide of public opinion was firmly on the side of the horse. A young man named Charles Irvine was standing on the road near Auchincloch Farm, by Kilsyth, when he saw three canal boats racing towards Wyndford lock. Two steamboats level with one another were just behind a traditional boat pulled by two horses. The horses were running at a fair pace, though it was difficult to make out for certain whether the driver was using his whip. Irvine saw the horses on their arrival at Wyndford, by which time one of the animals had froth coming out of its mouth and it refused to eat its food. Andrew Tripney called the accused's treatment of the horses unnecessary and cruel, while a third witness, James Reynolds, said the horses were going at a terrible rate. Canal banksman Andrew McIntosh had been working between Wyndford and the jetty house at Kelvinhead when the accused passed. He was running his horses fast in order to get to the lock before the steamers. McIntosh saw him giving the brown horse he was riding a lash. The banksman said in response to questioning that overdriving was "a thing that is done every day". He did not think that these horses had been treated brutally, but they had been driven too fast in order to get to the lock first; a boat arriving behind another at the lock was likely to be in for a long wait.

Perhaps the most authoritative evidence against Campbell came from Inspector Gibb, who was stationed at Stirling. Gibb had been cycling along the road towards Kilsyth. Opposite Kelvinhead Farm he had noticed a canal boat drawn by two horses going towards the lock at Wyndford. He could tell that one was an old stagecoach horse while the brown one, on which the driver was seated, was of the kind used by travelling people. The driver was lashing the horse for all he was worth and the animal was struggling. He supposed that Campbell's idea was to reach the lock before the two steamboats close behind. Gibb went to visit the horses at the stable at Wyndford. The brown horse lay down, completely exhausted and sweating all over. It would take none of the food offered and Gibb's opinion was that it had been driven too hard. The accused denied racing and over-driving the horses. He had been barely a year driving on the canal but was familiar with horses from four years as a stableboy. The brown horse had had a touch of colic. The Justice, Mr Lawson, considered the case not as clear-cut as they would have liked, since the horse had probably been inadequate for work in the first place. However, there was some evidence against the accused of cruelty. Since this was his first offence the penalty would be five shillings or five days in prison.

In the long-term, cruelty towards canal horses died out. Technological innovation would make animal traction redundant. In the end, canal horses were sold off at public auctions throughout Scotland and it is to be hoped that in their final days these hard-worked animals were given better treatment. But it would be misleading to suggest that the end of horse cruelty means all's well that ends well and crime is a thing of the past. From post-industrialism to modernity, the evolving landscape would continue to offer opportunities to moonlight lurkers. Though suspected infanticide would be far less common, crime would endure in the shape of assaults, murders, thefts, sexual offences on the banks, suspected narrowboat prostitution and the disposal of guns and stolen goods in the water.

SOURCES

The main sources consulted are listed here. In criminal cases where the ultimate sentence was carried out, Alex Young's *Encyclopaedia of Scottish Executions* proved to be particularly useful and for historical information, Jean Lindsay's *The Canals of Scotland* provided valuable background.

Items from the National Records of Scotland

Precognition against John Bruce, Alexander McArthur, Charles Stewart, Arthur Corner (AD14/38/461) and *Trial Papers* (JC26/1838/477).
Indicted for trial: Charles Campbell (JC26/1799/40); Charles Campbell, *Entry in West Circuit Minute Book* (JC13/31).
Precognition against Donald Davidson (AD14/22/152) and *Trial Papers* (JC26/1822/83).
John Davies, *Entry in North Circuit Minute Book* (JC11/54).
Precognition against Adam Johnston (AD14/44/329) and *Trial Papers* (JC26/1844/450).
Precognition against Bell MacMenemy, Hugh Richardson, Charles Hill, Thomas Connor (AD14/28/84) and *Trial Papers* (JC26/1828/305).
Trial Papers respecting Alexander McRae (JC26/1841/400).
Precognition against William Roughead (AD14/61/231) and *Trial Papers* (JC26/1861/209); *Precognition* against George Easton, Benjamin Nicol, William Roughead (AD14/50/283 1850); *Precognition* against Edward Quin (as witness), John MacKeown (as witness), Hugh MacKeown, Charles Clark, John MacGraddy, John Curran (AD14/26/277).
Precognition against Gavin Scott (AD14/18/55).
Entry, West Circuit Minute Book, Duncan MacArthur (JC13/33).

Note on the Edinburgh and Glasgow Union Canal Conspiracy

In the late 1820s an aggregate committee was formed by the Edinburgh and Glasgow Union Canal Company to investigate the allegations against Captain Cheyne. Between 1929 and 1931 the aggregate committee produced reports setting out the accusations against the clerk, an account of the extraordinary proceedings at a special general meeting on August 5th, 1829, and excerpts from George Beeby's diary. The accusations were answered by responses from Cheyne and proprietor George McCallum. These documents are held at the University of Glasgow and the National Library of Scotland. Also relevant are the *Rules and Regulations for Traders and Trackers on the Edinburgh and Glasgow Union Canal* (Edinburgh 1826).

The following were consulted, held by the National Records of Scotland:

Inventory of the Personal Estate of Hugh Baird (SC67/36/11 Stirling Sheriff Court, 1929).
Inventory of the Personal Estate of George Moncreiff (SC70/1/27 Edinburgh Sheriff Court Inventories, 1822).
The Telford Papers, at the Institution of Civil Engineers, offered personal and technical information, especially *To TT from George Moncreiff re Engagement of Contractors for Union Canal* (T/EG.175), *To TT from George Moncreiff re Problems with Hughes and Williams and Whittaker, Edinburgh & Glasgow Union Canal* (T/EG.217) and *To TT from William Hughes, Inverness, re his nephew Thomas' contracts on Union Canal* (T/EG.210).

Books and articles

Adams, Norman, *Scottish Bodysnatchers*, True Accounts (Goblinshead, Musselburgh, 2002).
Bowman, John Eddowes, *The Highlands and Islands A Nineteenth-Century Tour* (Alan Sutton, Gloucester, 1986).
Clelland, James, *Enumeration of the Inhabitants of the City of Glasgow and County of Lanark* (John Smith and Son, Glasgow, 1832).
Cameron, AD, *The Caledonian Canal* (Birlinn Limited, Edinburgh, 2005).

Clyde, Robert, *From Rebel to Hero The Image of the Highlander 1745 to 1830* (Tuckwell Press, East Linton, 1995).

Deas, George, Dunbar, W H and Robinson, James, *The Scottish Jurist: Containing Reports of Cases Decided in the House of Lords, Courts of Session, Teinds, and Exchequer, and the Jury and Justiciary Courts, No. 308 John Malcolm, Baird's Executor-Creditor, Pursuer v The West Lothian Railway Company, Defender, 10 June 1835* (M Anderson, Edinburgh, 1835).

Devine, T M, *The Scottish Clearances a History of the Dispossessed 1600-1900* (Allen Lane, 2018).

Dowds, T J, *The Forth and Clyde Canal A History* (Tuckwell Press, East Linton, 2003).

Edwards, Owen Dudley, *Burke and Hare* (Mercat Press, Edinburgh, 1993).

Fife, Malcolm, *The Story of Calton Jail Edinburgh's Victorian prison* (The History Press, Stroud, 2016).

Lennox, Suzie, *Bodysnatchers: Digging up the Untold Stories of Britain's Resurrection Men* (Pen and Sword History, South Yorkshire, 2016).

Lindsay, Jean, *The Canals of Scotland* (David and Charles, Newton Abbot, 1968).

Macmillan, Hugh P, *Adventures of a Paper Sleuth* (Penumbra Press, Ontario, 2004).

Meek, Donald E, *Early Steamship Travel from the Other Side: An 1829 Gaelic Account of the Maid of Morvern* (Ninteenth Century Studies, March 2013).

Moore, John, *Glasgow, Mapping the City* (Birlinn, Edinburgh, 2015).

Pallister, Marian, *The Crinan Canal* (Birlinn, Edinburgh, 2016).

Ransom, P J G, *Scotland's Inland Waterways* (P J G Ransom and NMS Publishing Ltd, Edinburgh, 1999).

Rosner, Lisa, *The Anatomy Murders* (University of Pennsylvania Press, Philadelphia, 2010).

Syme, David, *Reports of Proceedings in the High Court of Justiciary 1826-1829: James Glen pp. 264-280, W Burke and H M'Dougal pp. 345-396* (Edinburgh, M. Anderson, 1929).

Young, Alex F, *The Encyclopaedia of Scottish Executions 1750 to 1963* (Eric Dobby, Kent, 1998).

Newspapers

The following report the bodies of deceased infants found in or alongside canals in Scotland:

Aberdeen Evening Express (September 1893).
Aberdeen Herald and General Advertiser (April 1844).
Aberdeen Press and Journal (November 1827, April 1844, April 1858, July 1881, March 1923, September 1926, March 1923, March 1933, October 1936).
Airdrie and Coatbridge Advertiser (August 1904).
Banffshire Journal and General Advertiser (May 1858, March 1859).
Caledonian Mercury (January 1834, July & September 1837, July 1840, August & July 1842, April 1844, November 1846, November 1849, November 1856, October 1863, October 1865).
Dundee Advertiser (March 1866).
Dundee Courier (October 1836, April & July 1873, June 1873, March 1881, March 1883, June 1885, September 1893, December 1901, March 1903, April 1933, October 1936).
Dundee Evening Post (April 1903).
Dundee Evening Telegraph (May 1878, June 1879, July 1880, February 1882 February 1884, January 1889, April 1930, August 1938).
Dundee People's Journal (May 1916).
Dundee, Perth and Cupar Advertiser (November 1856).
Edinburgh Evening Courant (July 1851, March 1862, July 1869, April 1875, April 1876).
Edinburgh Evening News (July 1875, January 1876, January & September 1877, December 1878, July 1879, March 1884, May 1896, December 1897, July 1899, March 1902, April 1903, May 1916, October 1918).
Elgin Courier (April 1858).
Falkirk Herald (November 1856, October 1858, June & September 1860, June 1862, July 1869, November 1876, June 1884, June & September 1885, August 1886, June 1888, April 1903, April 1908, October 1927).
Glasgow Evening Citizen (March 1866).

Glasgow Evening Post (January 1879, August 1886).

Glasgow Herald (June 1862, October 1863, March 1864, October 1865, June 1876, March, June & December 1878, July 1879, August 1884, April 1900).

Glasgow Free Press (May 1860).

Glasgow Sentinel (April 1861, April 1865).

Greenock Advertiser (March 1847, October 1859).

Greenock Telegraph and Clyde Shipping Gazette (March 1903).

Inverness Courier (January 1834, April-March 1858).

John o'Groat Journal (January 1864).

Kilsyth Chronicle (August 1905, February 1916).

Kirkintilloch Gazette (July & September 1905).

Linlithgowshire Gazette (October 1930).

Milngavie and Bearsden Herald (May 1916).

Montrose, Arbroath and Brechin Review (September 1864, April 1916).

Nairnshire Telegraph (March 1858).

Northwich Guardian (December 1878).

Paisley and Renfrewshire Gazette (March 1878).

Paisley Herald and Renfrewshire Advertiser (January 1863, April 1869, April 1875)

Perthshire Courier (October 1810, July 1822).

The Scotsman (March 1847, June 1860, October 1863, March 1864, May 1878, October 1881, July 1895, July 1899, August 1900, August 1913, November 1928, April 1931, March 1933, July & September 1934, July 1935, February 1936).

Stirling Observer (April 1844, September 1845, September 1860).

Stonehaven Journal (November 1859, March 1862).

Southern Reporter (March 1864, July 1869).

Sunday Post (January 1927).

For the other types of crime, contemporaneous articles in the following newspapers were consulted:

Aberdeen Press and Journal
Belfast Commercial Chronicle

Bell's Life in London and Sporting Chronicle
Caledonian Mercury
Daily Telegraph and Courier (London)
Dundee Advertiser
Dundee Courier
Dundee Evening Telegraph
Durham County Advertiser
Edinburgh Evening Courant
Edinburgh Evening News
Evening Mail
Falkirk Herald
Fife Herald
Glasgow Evening Citizen
Glasgow Evening Post
Glasgow Free Press
Glasgow Herald
Glasgow Morning Journal
Glasgow Sentinel
Greenock Advertiser
Greenock Telegraph and Clyde Shipping Gazette
Inverness Courier
John o'Groat Journal
Leeds Intelligencer
London Courier and Evening Gazette
Morning Chronicle
Morning Post
Northern Whig
Paisley Herald and Renfrew Advertiser
Perthshire Courier
Saunders's Newsletter
The Scots Magazine
The Scotsman
Stirling Observer
Southern Reporter
Western Times

INDEX

Aberdeen 102-106, 154, 162-163
Aberdeen University 103
Aberdeenshire 11, 47-48
Aberdeenshire Canal 47, 101
Anderson, John 96
Anderston 15, 77
Argyll 95, 111-112
Askern, James 110
Auchindarroch 95

Baird, Hugh 94, 144-145, 147, 160-161
Bank of Scotland 60, 62-63
Barossa Inn, 130
Barr, Adam 24-25, 29
Barton, William 98-99
Bell, Joseph 93
Bishopbriggs 19, 100
Black Wood 95-96
Black, Hector 95-96, 113, 133-136, 166
Blaney, Mary 86
Bourhill, Euphenia 20-22, 23, 89-90
Brannan, John 99
Bridgeton 123
Brighton Wharf 151
Broadfoot, John 15, 18, 89
Broomielaw 121, 126, 131
Brown, Isabella 107
Brown, William 116, 122
Broxburn 99, 151
Bryce, George 92, 107-111
Bryceland, Bernard 35-36
Buchanan Street Station 26
Burke and Hare 110, 140-142, 161

Cadder 100, 140
Cairnbaan 95, 97, 111, 115
Caledonian Canal 47-48, 91 101, 130, 137, 160
Caledonian Railway 21, 26-27
Calton Jail 110, 161
Camelon 39-40
Campbell, Angus 15
Candleriggs 14
Canongate 144
Carron Company, 142
Carron Works 40, 47
Causewayend Bridge 89
Cheyne, Captain Alexander 93-94 143-153, 157-158, 160
Clyde Tube Works 67
Clydebank 117
Coatbridge 155, 162
Coatbridge. 30-31
Craig Glass 95
Crinan 11-12
Crinan Canal 95, 111, 125, 131, 138, 161, 166
Cross Keys Inn 32
Crown Works 67-68
Cruickshank, John 102
Cummings, James 137-138

Daily Mail 19
Dalmuir 116
Davidson, Donald 130, 159
Davies, Thmoas 137-138, 142, 159
Dewar, Donald 113
Dobbie's Loan 23, 26, 28
Doyle, Sir Arthur Conan 115
Dumfries 98

Duncan, Jane 105
Dunvegan 129

Eagle Inn 126-127, 129
Easton, John 149-152, 159
Edinburgh 20-22, 36-37, 49, 52,
    54-57, 59-62, 64-65, 71-72
    101, 110, 114-115, 119,
    129, 134, 136, 140-143,
    145, 147, 148, 151, 154,
    159-162, 164
Edinburgh University, 119

Falkirk 19, 23, 32, 37, 40, 42-43,
    52, 54, 59, 71, 75, 100, 120,
    144, 150, 162, 164
Falkirk Herald 23, 40, 75
Firhill Foundry 28
Forbes, Ann 91, 102-103, 105,
    106
Forbes, William 150
Fort Augustus 137
Fort William
Forth and Clyde Canal 9, 12-14,
    18, 23, 39, 47, 49, 59-60,
    71-75, 81, 86, 98-101, 116,
    140, 142,
Fox, John 38-39

Gallacher, William 67, 69
Gallagher, Bernard 28-29
Gallowgate 82, 83
Gartsherrie 151
Stephen, George 102-105
Glasgow 12, 14-15, 19, 21, 23,
    27-29, 31, 32, 35-37, 48-49,
    51, 64, 69, 72-74, 81, 83-87
Glasgow Daily Herald 81
Glasgow Herald 36

Glasgow, Paisley and Ardrossan
    Canal 121
Glassford Street 128
Glen, James 48, 71, 82-86
Glengarry 48
Gogar Station 107
Gorbals 94, 122, 128
Grangemouth 32, 40, 60, 142, 156
Grassmarket 37-38
Gray, James (Earl Grey) 22-23
Great North of Scotland Railway
    102

Haldane, James 130
Hankinson, Edith 99
Hannah, George 98
Holmes, Sherlock 93
Hope Street 142-143
Hunter, Charles Conway 115, 117,
    119
Huntly 102

Improvement 134
Infanticide 10, 76, 81, 84, 86
Inner Hebrides 120
Inverary 96-97
Inverness 101, 130-131, 160,
    163-164
Inverurie 101-102
Ireland 21, 27, 57, 58, 101, 120
Ironson, G H 140, 142
Irvine, Alex 103

John Watson and Son 14

Keenan Elizabeth 73, 76-81
Kelly, Thomas Mure 100
Kilmichael 138
Kilsyth 145, 156, 163

Kingscavel 150-151
Kinnaird, David 153, 157
Kintore murder 91
Kintore Murder, The 104

Lanarkshire 100, 145
Latona Incident, The 13, 142
Laurieston, Thomas 122
Lawrie, Agnes 101
Learmonth's Public House 62
Leith 66, 107, 151
Libberton's Wynd 110
Linlithgow 22, 23, 52, 54-55, 62,
        70-71, 73, 133-135, 141,
        146, 149-150
Linlithgow and Stirlingshire Hunt
        93
Linlithgow Gazette 70
Liverpool 142-143
Lochgilphead 95-97, 111-112,
        126, 131, 138
Lochmaddy 130
London 127, 164
Lord Aitchison 118-119
Lord Meadowbank 101, 123-124,
138

MacArthur, Alexander 95-97, 134-
        136, 138, 159
MacArthur, Duncan 95, 159
MacIntosh, Marjory 101
Majendie, Colonel Vivian Dering
        27, 29, 90
Maryhill 26, 28, 71, 73, 82, 90
McCall, Reverend William 31,
        52-58, 72
McComb, Margaret 73, 82-85
McCormack, Margaret 99
McCue, Mary 32-33
McCulloch, Peter 113-114

McDonald, Catherine 126
McDonald, Robert 132
McGeney, Henry 41-44
McGraddy, John 13, 55-59
McIntosh, Donald 101
McKinnon, Alexander 95-96, 120-
        123, 166, 167
McKinnon, Elizabeth 95
McLean, Rev James 129
McMenemy, Isabella (Bell) 11, 94,
        121-123
McNaughton, James 70-71
McRae, Alexander 101, 159
Methven 129
Mid Calder 20
Milne, Mary 102, 104
Monkland Canal 12, 32, 48-49, 52,
        67, 86, 155
Mooney, Charles 32-36
Morehead, John 60-61
Muiravonside 52, 55
Muiravonside Parish Church 140
Munn, James 93, 111-115
Murphy, Catherine 98
Murray, George 23-24, 30
Musselburgh 15

Napoleonic Wars 130, 132
Neptune's Staircase 48
Newhaven 65
Nobel Explosives 27
North Queensferry 107

Paisley and Ardrossan Canal 76-77
Paton, Andrew 148-150, 152
Peninsular War 145
Perth 130, 162
Phrenology 110
Port Dundas 14-15, 29, 32, 63, 71,
        86, 89, 98, 154

Port Eglinton 121
Port Elphinstone 101-103, 105
Port Hopetoun 36, 52, 141, 145, 147-150
Possil Road Aqueduct 90
Preston Fields 94
Professor Glaister 118
Professor Haycock 110
Professor Sydney Smith 119
Pyper, Eliza 105

Quin, Edward 55-58

Rape 100-101
Ratho 22-23, 92
Ratho Station 108
Riddell, Sir James 134
Ross, James 39-45, 61, 62, 64
Rottenrow 76
Roughead, William 30, 32-34
Rowan, Mary 111-113, 128
Royal Artillery 24
Royal Bank 127
Royal Engineers 145, 147
Royal Infirmary 119
Royal Navy 127-128

Scally, Mary 75-76
Scots Magazine, The 147, 164
Scotsman, The 76, 153, 163-164
Scott, Gavin 51-52
Seaton, Jeannie 92, 107, 109-110
Sherriffhall 151
Shillinglaw, James 148, 151
Ship Bank 128-130
Simpson, John 114
Sinclair, James 100
Skye 129
Smith, William 101

Society for the Prevention of Cruelty to Animals 153-154
South Uist 130-132
Springburn 100
Standalane Cottage 116
Stephen, George 91
Stevenson, Robert Louis 106
Stewart, Charles 129-130, 134-136, 159
Stirling 43, 54, 56-57, 59
Stirlingshire 37, 60
Stockbridge, 143, 147
Stonehaven Journal 76

Taylor, Elizabeth 17, 52, 57
Telford, Thomas 137, 160
Tennent, Rae 100
Thainston Woods 102, 105
The Strange Case of Dr Jekyll and Mr Hyde 107
Thistle Bank 128
Thomas Davies 137
Thomson, John 105
Thomson, Margaret 105
The Times, 27
Tippermuir 130
Tiree 120-121
Todd, Margaret 109
Todd, Robert 107
Tolbooth 52
Tradeston Gasworks 23, 26
Turnbull, James 22-23

Union Canal 11, 12, 20, 22, 36, 46, 52, 54, 59-62, 65, 70-75, 89, 94, 99, 101, 107, 133, 140-141, 143, 144, 146, 153-154, 158-160
Union Canal Company 60

Van Diemens Land 10

Waddell, Alexander 48-52
Walkingdon Farm 97
Water Street 98
Waterloo Fund, 129
Wilkie, William 62-64
Wilson, James 14-18, 78-80
Wilson, William 108
World War Two 70
Wyse, James 150-151

ALSO FROM RYMOUR BOOKS

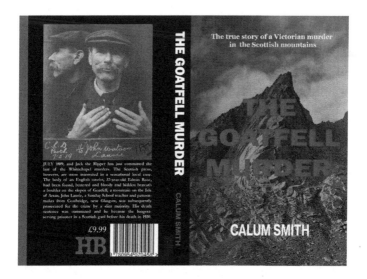

This is the true story of an infamous murder in the Scottish mountains. Taking place in 1898, the year Jack the Ripper committed the last of his murders, the murder of an English tourist, Edwin Rose, on Goatfell, in the Isle of Arran, was a sensation of the time.

Calum Smith's new study unearths previously hidden evidence and exposes the brutality of the Scottish judicial and penal establishment of the time.

'A work of outstanding research', DENNIS GRAY

https://www.rymour.co.uk

ALSO FROM RYMOUR BOOKS

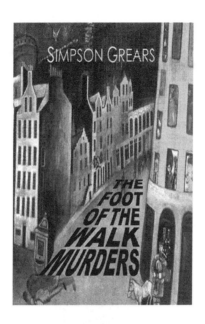

https://www.rymour.co.uk

RYMOUR BOOKS

poetry • history • debate